M000218226

SEIDR: THE GATE IS OPEN

For Harriet, Lavinia, Carol, and Astrid.
Sisters, Mothers, Grandmothers, Daughters

And of course Freyja of the falcon cloak

ABOUT THE AUTHOR

Katie Gerrard is a writer, researcher and workshop facilitator with a passion for the magic of the Runes and Seidr. She has been studying the different forms of Norse magic and working with the Norse Gods since discovering them in the 1990s, when she was at university in West Wales.

Katie lectures and facilitates workshops at national and international events on the Runes, Seidr and related subjects, and also leads a practical Seidr group on the outskirts of London. Her work on the runes spans understanding, divination, voice work, and runic magic, which she teaches in and around London (UK). Her work on Seidr focuses on the High Seat rite and her essay 'The Seer' on this subject appeared in the anthology *Priestesses Pythonesses Sibyls*. She is the author of *Odin's Gateways*, which is a practical guide to the wisdom of the Runes through Galdr, Sigils and Casting.

When she is not doing things of a magickal persuasion she enjoys creative pursuits such as fashion design, sewing, and various handicrafts. She lives in London with her husband, daughter, and fat idiot cat.

Other books by Katie Gerrard

- *Odin's Gateways*, A practical guide to the wisdom of the Runes through Galdr, Sigils and Casting, Avalonia, 2009

- *Priestesses Pythonesses & Sibyls* (contributor), Collection of modern experiential essays by women, edited by Sorita d'Este, Avalonia, 2009

- *Vs.* (contributor), Anthology of essays on the subject of polarity in mythology and modern Pagan practices, edited by Kim Huggens, Avalonia, 2011

For more information see:

www.avaloniabooks.co.uk
or
www.thebirchtree.com

Published by Avalonia

BM Avalonia
London
WC1N 3XX
England, UK

www.avaloniabooks.co.uk

Seidr: The Gate is Open
Copyright © Katie Gerrard 2011

Design by Avalonia.

ISBN-10: 1-905297-52-1
ISBN-13: 978-1-905297-52-8

First Edition, February 2011

Cover Art – The Gate is Open by Laura Daligan © 2011

British Library Cataloguing in Publication Data. A catalogue record for this book is available from the British Library.

All rights reserved. No part of this publication may be reproduced or utilized in any form or by any means, electronic or mechanical, including photocopying, microfilm, recording, or by any information storage and retrieval system, or used in another book, without written permission from the authors.

SEIDR

THE GATE IS OPEN

WORKING WITH TRANCE PROPHECY,
THE HIGH SEAT,
AND NORSE WITCHCRAFT

BY

KATIE GERRARD

PUBLISHED BY AVALONIA
WWW.AVALONIABOOKS.CO.UK

ACKNOWLEDGEMENTS

This book has been a long time in coming so my first thanks go to my nearest and dearest for putting up with the endless planning, plotting and researching; especially to my husband Gareth and daughter Astrid.

My second thank you must go to all of those who have been right there with me, adding ideas, trying out my crazy plans, and making those *'ah ha moment'* suggestions. From those, like Ross Brazier who were there right at the very beginning, through to the late Leila Wiberg whose suggestions formed an integral part of the high seat rite given in this book, and not forgetting Marielle Holman who has been instrumental in my most recent seidr rites.

A special thank you must go to those whose research and information helped me to form my work, authors such as Jan Fries, Diana Paxson, Galina Lindqvist, and Jenny Blain. Their work has widened the scope and understanding of seidr.

Thank you also to my publishers Sorita d'Este and David Rankine who have patiently waited through many writes, rewrites and vast overhauls, and were even patient through my creative forgetfulness to post contracts.

Lastly, thank you to my faithful proof readers and to the talented Laura Daligan who once again has come up with an iconic image for the cover.

TABLE OF CONTENTS

INTRODUCTION 9

THE VOLVA 31
THE SEER 49
THE SORCERESS 61
THE HIGH SEAT 79
THE DEAD 123
THE OTHER 136
THE GODS 148
SEIDR IN ANTIQUITY 162
CONTEMPORARY SEIDR 179
CONCLUSION 195

FURTHER READING 197
BIBLIOGRAPHY 199

Cover Art by Laura Daligan.
**Find out more about Laura and her artwork by visiting:
www.lauradaligan-art.com**

SEIDR: THE GATE IS OPEN

INTRODUCTION

The Gate is Open has been many long years in preparation. Almost from the moment I started working with the High Seat Rite I had a feeling that this book was calling to me to write it. Over a decade later and through many different formats and rewrites, here it is. I feel I should add an apology here to those who have been waiting years to either publish or read it! The first time I saw the word seidr being used was a brief mention in Kveldulf Gundarsson's *Teutonic Religion.*[1] It was 1997 and I was in my first year of university and just starting to get acquainted with paganism. There was a lot of information available about paganism, Druidry, and Wicca, and also about heathenry and the northern traditions. When it came to seidr, it seemed almost impossible to locate anything concrete that explained what to do and how to do it, especially aimed at the beginner. Despite the fact that the term was being used in the wider pagan world[2] and Jan Fries' book *Seidways* had been published the year before, it seemed impossible to find out anything more about the contemporary use of the word. At that point, Jan Fries' book was almost impossible to locate. Whether it was the elusiveness of the term that excited me, or whether it was the concept of a Northern Tradition female centred

---

[1] Gundarsson, *Teutonic Religion: Folk Beliefs and Practices of the Northern Tradition.* 1993.
[2] Jordan, *Witches: An Encyclopedia of Paganism and Magic.* 1996.

tradition, the desire to find out more was awakened in me, and my journey was to begin.

As 1997 progressed, more and more information began to become available. Diana Paxson's article *The Return of the Volva*[3] was available to me through the internet, and I located *Seidways* on inter library loan shipped in from deepest East Anglia. (*Seidways* was republished a year later and is now widely available). Further ahead in time, Jenny Blain's *Nine Worlds of Seid Magic*[4] was published in 2001. Throughout these years, I was unable to meet anyone that was already working with seidr. Instead I turned to every primary and secondary source on seidr that was available to me and pieced together rites. These have developed over the years and been added to as more and more people have been kind enough to allow me to share my experiences with them and make suggestions.

The overriding purpose of *The Gate is Open* is to share my experiences with a wider audience. These rites and rituals have been developed very much as part of the wider pagan community, whether that has been at conferences, private events, or with the small pagan groups that I have been a part of over the years. Seidr by its very nature is difficult to define, partly because we don't have a large amount of information about the seidr of the past, but also because in modern practice the word is used to describe so many different things. Due to this, *The Gate is Open* is not a definitive guide to the practice, merely one person's work.

The Gate is Open is designed predominantly as a practical book for those who want to learn from and experience my path to the Seer. Whether you have been involved in shamanic and spiritual religions for many years, or are just starting out, and whether you work individually or as part of a group, you will hopefully find that this book will both serve as a guide to piecing together your own spiritual practice, and will give you a collection of rites and ideas that are being successfully worked by others.

Although this is a practical book, much of it is taken up with information I have found through researching the subjects along the way. This information is included to ensure that my thought processes and the sources I have used are clearly identifiable to my readers who want to find

---

[3] Paxson, *The Return of the Volva*.1993.
[4] Blain, *Nine Worlds of Seid-Magic.* 2001.

out more information or who want to make sure that they understand where different ideas have come from. Although this veers the format slightly into the academic and ethnographic, the reader is encouraged to be under no illusions to the purpose of the book, which is for a modern pagan practitioner to share with other modern pagan practitioners. To give simply the rites would be to take away from the journey that birthed them and would deprive the reader of the ability to decide for themselves the validity of the primary and secondary sources that went into their creation. This is a spiritual journey laid bare for an audience who are either already treading a similar path or are looking for guidance in order to follow a well trodden path to a similar end point. In anthropological terms, I have not *'gone native'*, for I have never been anything but *'native'*. I am so native that I will never be able to produce a document about my spiritual work that stands up to rigorous academic scrutiny, therefore I ask you, as a reader, to understand this and to see *The Gate is Open* for what it is, an account by a practitioner sharing their knowledge. Firstly, I am a practitioner, secondly a guide and a teacher, thirdly a folklorist and historian, and lastly, an anthropologist.

The reader, as a practitioner accessing this information will find that this does not take the form of a step by step workbook. Instead, these are a series of individual rites that can be accessed and experimented with one by one, or by taking elements from specific rites and ideas and building a practice that works for you. Some of these rites are suitable for individuals; some have suggestions on how they can be adapted for individuals, but the majority of these practical rites have been developed for small groups. As with most group and team work, you will have better results working within groups of people that you are comfortable with and have worked with before (and feel comfortable working at a high energy ritual level with). If you are a small group forming in order to take on these rites, I would recommend that you undertake celebratory rites and get to know and understand how you gel spiritually as a group before you attempt the majority of the rites in this book.

11

WHAT IS SEIDR?

The term *'seidr'* comes from literature written in Scandinavia between the tenth and twelfth centuries. These tales from the Viking and pre-Christian north give us the word seidr, which is often used to describe supernatural activity. It has been suggested that the word *seidr* within the Old Norse literature is interchangeable with the word witch, used in a similar way within British medieval literature,[5] although the term witch has also been used within the Norse literature.[6] In the same way that it is incredibly difficult to find a definition for the term *'witch'* (or even for witchcraft, magic, and ritual), it is difficult to universally define seidr. Another word that has been used and is often used within translations of the *Sagas* is sorcery.[7] As such, although there are many similar themes which run through the examples the *Sagas* give of seidr, there are also many differences.

The word *seidr* is pronounced *'Seeth'* or *'Sayth'* with the *'d'* replacing the Old Norse character *'ð'* which is pronounced as *'th'*. The word can be seen spelt as *seid, seidhr, seith, seithr*, and in the Swedish as *sejd*.[8] The root of the word seidr has been vastly debated by heathens. Diana Paxson[9] suggests that the word seidr relates to *'sing'* or *'speak'*. This links it with the Norse word galdr which refers to a song or incantation. She also links it to the word *sit* and to the word *séance*[10] which brings images of spiritualism and mediums. Sheena McGrath suggests that seidr is linked to the old English word *sieðe* (which translates into modern English as *seethe*),[11] firstly meaning to boil (e.g. seething water on the stove), but secondly (and more commonly used in the modern English language) to get silently and slowly angry. Edred Thorsson refutes this theory and points out that the Old Norse word for seethe is

---

5 Morris, *Sorceress or Witch: Image of Gender in Mediaeval Iceland and Northern Europe.* 1991.
6 Dubois, *Nordic Religions in the Viking Age.* 1999.
7 Chisholm & Flowers (eds), *A Source-book of Seid.* 2002.
8 Strömbäck et al., *Sejd: och andra studier i nordisk själsuppfattning.* 2000.
9 Paxson, *The Return of the Volva.* 1993.
10 Ibid.
11 McGrath, *Asyniur: Women's Mysteries in the Northern Tradition.* 1997.

sjóða[12] which gives a very different translation. This is a very good point, but further investigation into the word brings us to the Norse word *syð* which translates as to boil.[13] This is incredibly close to the Old English *sieðe*. However, the similarity between the words does not categorically prove that they are from the same root source and in order to come to this conclusion, more evidence will need to be found to back up this theory.

Edred Thorsson also links the word seidr with wiccecraft (wicce being pronounced witch and being the Old English word for female Witch).[14] He also links the word with the modern German *wicken* which means '*to practice soothsaying*',[15] as well as to the Old English word *siðsa* which he gives as meaning a '*kind of bewitching*'.[16] A similar term used in the Norse is *siða* which is '*to perform sorcery*'.[17]

Examples of words used in this book that come from the root word seidr are:

- Seidkona (seiðkona) a female seidr worker, also referred to as volva[18]
- Gydia (gyðia) a priestess[19]
- Seidrmann (seiðman) a male seidr worker[20]
- Seidhjallr (seiðhjallr) the seidr platform (or high seat)

The literature that the terminology is mostly found within is a collection of ancient Icelandic stories often referred to as '*the Sagas*' and '*the Eddas*'. The *Sagas* are (often family based) heroic tales and include *Sagas* such as *Erik the Red*,[21] *Egil's Saga*,[22] *Laxdaela Saga*,[23] and *Olaf's*

---

[12] Thorsson, *Witchdom of the True*. 1999.
[13] Chisholm & Flowers (eds), *A Source-book of Seid*. 2002.
[14] Thorsson, *Witchdom of the True*. 1999.
[15] Ibid.
[16] Ibid.
[17] Chisholm & Flowers (eds), *A Source-book of Seid*. 2002.
[18] Fries, *Seidways: Shaking, Swaying & Serpent Mysteries*. 1996.
[19] Chisholm & Flowers (eds), *A Source-book of Seid*. 2002.
[20] Ibid.
[21] Jones, *Erik the Red and Other Icelandic Sagas*. 1961.
[22] Eiriksson, *Egil's Saga*. 2004.
[23] Magnusson et al., *Laxdaela Saga*, 1975.

Saga.[24]   By the *'Eddas'* we are referring to what can be considered to be the most widely read primary source on Norse mythology – the *Prose* and *Poetic Eddas*.   Snorri Sturluson's *Edda* (also known as the *Prose* or *Younger Edda*) was written in around 1200 and is a collection of stories about the Norse Gods.   Snorri Sturluson was a Christian priest so it is unclear how much he may have been influenced by Christian ideas and mythology.   The *Poetic Edda* is a collection of Norse poems, contained within the *Codex Regis* manuscript, written in 13th century Iceland.[25] Although the *Poetic Edda* was written around the same time as Snorri's *Edda*, the *Poetic Edda* is considered to be compiled from older traditional sources, hence its alternative name of the *Elder Edda*.

In finding a definition of seidr within antiquity, it is important to look at what each of the accounts spoken about as seidr have in common (and what they don't). Firstly, although some accounts refer to seidr as being feminine and *'unmanly'*[26] there are as many accounts of male seidr workers as there are female, although the male accounts tend to be more focused on the sorcery and the female on the prophecy.[27] Secondly, all of the accounts are describing something that is supernatural (or outside of the normal and known.) Seidr affects the natural world in an unnatural way.   Thirdly, many accounts are focused on people, either providing a service for them or working against them.   Fourthly, the actions described as seidr are achieved mentally, or from afar. Seidr is described as being practiced while the body is still. In many accounts this is amplified with the use of a platform (the Seidhjallr). Lastly, all the accounts are of actions that are taken deliberately and within a measured and focused way.   These seidr accounts   describe   planned   and   often   ritualised supernatural   events,   not   accidental   or   coincidental supernatural events.

Perhaps the most famous modern day example of seidr within the *Sagas* is the action of using seidr to prophesise. In this example a seeress travels from farmstead to farmstead prophesising for the inhabitants.   The most

---

[24] Sturluson, *Heimskringla: The Chronicle of the Kings of Norway.* 2008.
[25] Larrington, *The Poetic Edda.* 1999.
[26] Blain, *Nine Worlds of Seid-Magic.* 2001.
[27] Jochens, *Old Norse Images of Women.* 1996.

famous example of this is found within the *Greenland Saga*[28] but it is also present in many others (for example *Landnamabok*, *Arrow-Odd's Saga*, and *King Hrolf Kraki's Saga*.[29] Another well known use of seidr is for cursing, and examples of nightmares (see chapter seven) can be found in *Laxdaela Saga*,[30] *Ynglingasaga*,[31] and *Egil's Saga*,[32] among others. In *Laxdaela Saga* for example, Kotkel lures his victim out of the safety of his house and once lured out his seidr magic is able to kill him. The third subject of seidr within the *Sagas* is of shape changing and astral travel, for example *Thidrek's Saga* describes a seidkona who can change herself into a lion and a dragon,[33] and *Volsungasaga* describes a sorceress and a woman changing shapes (or bodies). Although it has often been said that seidr is hostile[34] or aggressive magic, this is not always the case. Many accounts of seidr involve prophecy and these accounts (in particular the *Greenland Saga*)[35] are not seen as being hostile or aggressive in any way (although it should also be noted that occasionally an upset volva who has come to prophesise might get a little grumpy). There are also accounts of protective magic (see chapter seven). Therefore, to define seidr as hostile is not doing justice to it. As Galina Lindquist writes in *Shamanic Practices on the Urban Scene*, *"Seid was performed both with constructive and with destructive purposes, and the volva was a respected and feared member of the community."*[36]

This refers to the definition of seidr within antiquity, but what of defining seidr within modern pagan and heathen practice? By the nature of the word, modern seidr draws on the accounts given in the Norse literature of practices referred to as seidr. Yet for the seidr practitioner, this creates the very real problem that much of these accounts mention seidr in passing. It takes place as a sub

---

[28] Jones, *Erik the Red and Other Icelandic Sagas*. 1961.
[29] Chisholm & Flowers (eds), *A Source-book of Seid*. 2002.
[30] Magnusson et al., *Laxdaela Saga*. 1975.
[31] Snorri Sturluson, *Heimskringla or the Lives of the Norse Kings*. 2004.
[32] Eiriksson, *Egil's Saga*. 2004.
[33] Chisholm & Flowers (eds), *A Source-book of Seid*. 2002.
[34] Hilda Ellis Davidson.
[35] Jones, *Erik the Red and Other Icelandic Sagas*. 1961.
[36] Lindquist, *Shamanic Performances on the Urban Scene: Neo-shamanism in Contemporary Sweden*. 1997.

plot within a greater story and as such many of these accounts explain very little about how it was done, or where it originates. These accounts certainly don't give us a fully formed list of what constitutes as seidr and what does not. With this in mind, how can we seek to piece together rites and practices that use seidr without at least a little artistic license? And here becomes the problem, how much artistic license can you use and still be working seidr? Where do you borrow the missing pieces of the jigsaw from?

Modern day definitions of seidr will undoubtedly often link the word with shamanism or at least with shamanistic practices. I discuss this in greater detail in chapter nine, but it is clear to say that modern seidr practice can be seen as incredibly shamanistic. Jenny Blain says *"I locate seidr as ecstatic practice within specific cultural contexts".*[37] The term shaman has become a catch all term for ecstatic ritual that uses altered states (and often otherworld journeying), yet originally it was used to describe specific Siberian practice. Stephen Flowers and James Chisholm use the definition: *"In truth, seid is a complex form of magic, peculiar to the Scandinavians. It was certainly also exported to all the regions inhabited by the Norse in Britain and elsewhere."*[38] For me, I think the term *'seidr'* really has to be reserved for practices that are inspired by accounts given as seidr in the Norse literature. If we begin to include practices that are inspired by the word seidr in our definition, we have the likelihood of losing the term behind a myriad of practices that then begin to have little in common with each other. Sadly, this has already begun to happen. Flowers and Chisholm remind us that already a lot of what is described in modern heathenry as seidr is simply people *'dressing up'* their current practices in Norse regalia and calling it seidr. [39] It must also be remembered, however, that language is fluid, and in much the same way as shaman is a term easily misused, so is seidr, and using shaman as an example, it is a term that it is not copyrighted or rigorously defined. After all, the examples of seidr within antiquity are wide ranging enough. Therefore, there is nothing to stop the use of the term seidr in a wider context.

---

[37] Wallis, *Shamans/Neo-Shamans: Ecstasies, Alternative Archaeologies & Contemporary Pagans.* 2003.
[38] Chisholm & Flowers (eds), *A Source-book of Seid.* 2002.
[39] Ibid.

My definition of the term seidr for this book therefore becomes: Seidr is a term denoting supernatural actions within the Old Norse *Sagas* and is used in a similar way to the words *'sorcery'* and *'witchcraft'*. Seidr in modern practice therefore becomes rituals and actions that are inspired by the supernatural events referred to as seidr within the Old Norse literature.

> *"In many cases, the rituals were probably mysterious to the writers of the Sagas themselves, who may have learned of them from textual accounts or hearsay reports."*[40]

NORSE WITCHCRAFT

As a part of this book, I am looking at other seer and witchcraft rites that are practiced within the Norse cosmology and context. As discussed above, it is unhelpful to refer to everything that is witchcraft and shamanic within Norse spirituality as seidr, therefore some of the rites and examples given within this book are not collected under the title of seidr. However, they make a very relevant and informative addition to the material.

THE USE OF SOURCE MATERIALS

As an academically trained writer, it is important to me to consider the background of the primary and secondary sources I have used, as well as their likelihood to be unbiased or to hold theories that were common in the times they were written but have since been discounted.

I am aware that although some of these sources may be discredited by some due to bias or to new evidence coming forward that puts a question mark on the conclusions gained. However, as a practitioner, I am also aware that many of these sources are still extremely valid and viable when studying belief systems, or considering seer practices for practical study. While much of this book looks at reconstructing the original practice, I am aware that the stories we are working with are not practical guides, therefore there is a need to fill in the gaps and to

---

[40] Dubois, *Nordic Religions in the Viking Age.* 1999.

look to modern practice to build on what source material we have.

It is also important to remember that much of the source material I have used had been originally written as literature, as stories for children, or as folktales. There are many theories that build on the truth that lives behind folk stories and allegory, but the fictional aspect of these stories means that they are not written to be taken literally. However, fiction is often based on reality and belief and these sources hold a wealth of information that tells us about the time they were written in, and hints at possible beliefs that may have been held.

Where I am using material that has been widely questioned, I will make it clear which parts have been questioned or discredited in order to ensure that the reader is able to make their own mind up about the material within and how they choose to work with it. Many of the texts I have quoted are out of print, and some had small print runs as *'limited interest'* books. Due to this, many of them may be more difficult to get hold of. Over the last ten years of my research, more and more avenues have become available for reading this kind of text. Whereas, in the early days of research, I spent many years sitting in the reading room at the British Library, over the last few years electronic versions of out of print books, online article libraries, and basic reprints of the more popular out of print books have kept me working steadily at home in the warm.

I absolutely recommend trawling through the older texts. Some theories and information will be very much a product of its time, but it is worth remembering that the information presented currently is also a product of its time and however careful authors are, bias and popular ideas will still be present. By taking a step outside of the information written in the last thirty years, we are more likely to notice where bias appears and can take a step back and look at ideas that may have fallen out of favour now but that might have some merit to your personal work and theories.

TRANCE AND JOURNEYING

Trance is often thought of within Western culture to be an unconscious state.[41] In reality, a trance can be any level of altered consciousness. We often hear of people being put into hypnotic trances and being surprised at how much they remember, or how awake they were. Often you will hear someone not realising that they were in a trance. It is more helpful to consider trance to be an altered state of consciousness than it is to imagine a hypnotic *'one, two, three, you're under'* scenario. There are, however, different depths of trance states. Even within a fairly deep trance you might still be surprised how lucid you feel and how aware you are. Different levels of trance are useful for different tasks and it is worth experimenting. Sometimes the deepest trance might not be the one that you are most productive within. It is unusual for someone to be able to fall into a deep trance without either going through a lighter trance state first or without using *'triggers'*. By triggers[42] we are talking about certain actions that are done in a certain order that remind the consciousness that you want it to do a certain thing or behave in a certain way (in this instance, you want it to go into an altered or trance state). By including triggers in your rites, you are giving your subconscious clues about what to expect next and will find that, once you have used these triggers a certain amount of times, they will allow you to enter a deeper trance, more quickly.

Experience with trance work and an understanding of what you need to go into trance and what you need to come out of trance is essential for the majority of the rites included in this book. Trance and journeying is a subject that has been covered very well within various different books so it is not something that I will repeat in great depth here. For an in-depth introduction to working with trance, try Diane Paxson's *Trance-portation*.[43] Another classic guide is Michael Harner's *The Way of the Shaman*.[44] Journeying

---

41 Harner, *The Way of the Shaman*. 1992.

42 Ready and Burton, *Neuro-linguistic Programming (NLP) Workbook for Dummies*. 2008.

43 Paxson, *Trance-Portation: Learning to Navigate the Inner World*. 2008.

44 Harner, *The Way of the Shaman*. 1992.

is also covered briefly within my first book *Odin's Gateways.*[45]

The difference between a journey (otherwise called a pathworking) and a meditation tends to be that a meditation is concentrating on a fixed point or idea, whereas a journey takes you through different points and is often taken for a specific purpose and therefore involves some kind of quest. A trance journey can sometimes take you outside of your body, and this is a theme you will see often in this book. More often than not a journey/pathworking will help you to explore your inner realms, your subconscious and memory, and help you to work through decisions and problems.

The basic journey starts with stating the intent. For example *'I am going to journey to Asgard and meet with Odin'* or *'I am going to find out what will happen if I choose this path over the other one.'* You also need to give yourself a time limit. Being in trance is like any other kind of physical or mental challenge, you need to build up your tolerance gradually. Start low (if you have never done anything like this before you might even want to start with one or two minutes) and work up with practice. If you are a total beginner, it is worth trying a few guided (someone else talks or drums you through it) pathworkings before you go it alone. A common mistake with journeying is to assume that you have to *'see'* things to be experiencing them. The best journeys use all the senses (sight, sound, touch, taste, smell) but your primary sense while in an altered state might not be sight, you might experience via sound or smell before you begin to *'see'* things. The word *'visualise'* can be misleading, it isn't just about what you can and can't see.

There is no utilitarian *'best way'* to enter a trance or to move into a deeper trance state. Everyone is different and you will find what works best for you. The more you use these techniques the more they become triggers. Your subconscious will react to them faster and more effectively every time you use them. Of course, this doesn't mean that once you have used a certain trigger a few times, the correct altered state will be automatic for you. It is like any other skill, some people will be more adept at it than others and different people will need different times. If something doesn't seem to be working for you at all after you have

---

[45] Gerrard, *Odin's Gateways: A Practical Guide to the Wisdom of the Runes, Through Galdr, Sigils and Casting.* 2009.

given it a try enough times, change your tact and try something else.

Common techniques used to move the conscious into an altered state are:

- drumming
- dancing
- chanting
- music
- repetition
- exhaustion
- relaxation
- incense
- swaying
- pain
- sensory deprivation (for example, darkness)

Your best route into an altered state is likely to be a combination of these. Don't forget to try different things within these (for example different drum beats, speed of music/dance, volume, different kinds of incense).

BEFORE YOU START...

The last part of the introduction could be easily called *'the boring bit'*! The ideas and rites in this book are not suitable for complete beginners. This is not to say that you cannot include a complete beginner in one of these rites, nor is it to say that I insist that everyone attending my rites have intermediate and advanced skills in trance, journeying, and channelling. However, if you are working alone or working in a group that does not have any experienced members, you should ultimately seek to gain more experience in trance and journeying techniques before you attempt anything practical from the following chapters.

Even if you are an experienced practitioner of trance and ritual, it is worth reading through the next few sections and reviewing your techniques for keeping things safe. Seidr can be high energy work and as such it is essential for me to include practical and esoteric examples of what to do if things don't go according to plan. Perhaps even more importantly, always remember to ground and centre yourself and your practitioners when the rite ends. By this, I mean, remember to make sure that any excess energy and exuberance left in your practitioners at the end of the rite is fully released by them, and that anyone who has been in an altered state is fully back and present in their every day consciousness once the rite has finished, and especially, before you let them leave your presence and go back to their normal lives. The last section of the introduction will give you some ideas on making sure this happens.

PROTECTING

Protection within this kind of work is not about locking the doors and not letting anything through. After all, you don't want to shut the door on the entities you are waiting to speak to and work with. However, you don't want to put yourself and your attendees in a situation that can put them in spiritual or physical danger. Everyday health and safety obviously still applies and I don't need to take time to go over this area. Spiritual health and safety is just as important.

Perhaps the most well known way of protecting and containing energy within a rite is the Wiccan circle.[46] If this is known to you and works well for you, why not use it? There is a train of thought within heathenry that suggests that Wicca is so ingrained into modern paganism that it finds its way into rites that perhaps it doesn't have a place in. Sadly, this tends to be countered by the creation of rites to create a sacred space that vastly resemble the Wiccan circle.[47] Realistically, if it works for you, does it matter where it originated? However, if you have never used this technique, or you know that it doesn't work for you, why not look at your options and come up with something that does?

The first step in spiritual health and safety is making sure that the space you are working in is clean. This doesn't mean that it has to be sterile and soulless, but you do need to make sure that the energy feels right for the task and that you remove anything unnecessary or unhelpful. A classic technique is using salt and water and/or incense (Sage and Rosemary are both purifying and work very well) but there are a whole host of techniques that you can use.

---

[46] d'Este, *Towards the Wiccan Circle - A Practical Introduction to the Principles of Wicca.* 2008.
[47] Pennick, *Practical Magic in the Northern Tradition.* 1994.

I give an example of how you can create a sacred space using runes in *Odin's Gateways.*[48]

What are you protecting yourself from? One argument suggests that any high energy work creates a great ball of energy that lights your work up like stadium lights, calling to everything to come and play. The opposite argument states that very little actually notices or cares and more importantly, if you are working with spirits, don't you *want* a certain level of attendance? Both ideas are correct. If you have the music loud enough to attract gatecrashers, you don't want the doors swung wide open. But you don't want to make things so closed that the things you want to interact with can't get in. So there has to be a middle ground. There needs to be some kind of gateway or your protection needs to be flexible enough to make it easy for the things you want to work with to enter. The disir circle I give as an example in chapter four is a good compromise, but work out what works for you.

Most importantly, have your wits about you and make sure you check and double check if things feel right. Don't allow yourself to be tricked. Whatever you are dealing with, remember your manners by all means, but make sure that the entities remember theirs too: your rite, your rules. There is a school of thought that suggests that deities are bigger and stronger than us and therefore we need to let them do whatever they want. That they might be, but if they are in my space and my rite then they play by my rules, having said that, if I am in their realms, I need to play by their rules.

It is also useful to have an element of personal protection. Most beginner books on paganism (and even on new age thought) will give examples on how to keep your energy (or your aura) strong and full. You might also have entities that work to protect you (see chapter four), these are worth encouraging for as long as they are protecting you and not damaging you in any way.

KEEPING ORDER

Seidr is high energy work, coupled with techniques that may be new or complicated for some people. As such, if you are putting together a seidr rite for other people, it is

---

[48] Gerrard, *Odin's Gateways.* 2009.

important to know how to avoid things going wrong, and to know what to do if you or anyone else has any problems.

Firstly, set the ground rules before you start. Those that are new to magical practice won't necessarily know what is expected of them, and those that have experience won't know what you need from them for this particular rite.

Within the seer rites, everyone needs to remain focused which means that they come into the rite without any concerns that will affect their ability to concentrate, and that their dedication to the rite is 100%. If someone is not able to provide this to you then it is not the right time for them to be in a Seer rite. Be clear yourself on what the focus of the rite is, and what you expect of your attendees. For a high seat rite, your attendees are focused on the Seer and their energy goes towards the Seer. This is no time for channelling anything else, or journeying anywhere, or doing anything that has the likelihood to change or distract the energy of the rite. At the worst, something like this could put that practitioner, as well as the rest of the group in danger. The usual outcome is that the rite lacks energy and focus and therefore doesn't go as well as it should have done which is then a disappointment for everyone else present. Having said this, there are rites where a change of direction or unplanned events add to the energy and success of the rite. If this is part of the way you work, it might not be a problem, but whichever is acceptable for your rite, make sure that you make it clear in your instructions before the rite starts.

Don't be afraid to refuse to work with someone you don't feel comfortable with. It might seem harsh, but some magical workings are not for everyone. You don't have to refuse to work with them forever, it might be that a later date or within another rite you feel happier working with them. But trust your instincts and don't be afraid to say no to attendees. If someone has a history of severe mental illness or is physically unwell to the extent that a high energy seer rite might tire them out or cause them physical pain and discomfort, or if someone has had problems with trance and magical work in the past and not overcome them yet, then this kind of ritual might be best for them to avoid. Don't feel that you have to be inclusive at the detriment of your own safety and enjoyment of the rite and that of the rest of your participants. This is one of the reasons that the rites my group puts on are always *'invite'* rather than *'open'*. We want to share our traditions and let others experience the rites, but they will never be totally open events because then it becomes difficult to say no to people.

Whatever the experience level of your group, it is good to have one or more people who agree to not go fully into trance in order to keep an eye on the rest of the participants. This leaves the person who is leading the ritual free to concentrate on the Seer and the flow of the rite. Within the high seat rite, I have named this person *'the watcher'* and more details on this are available in chapter four.

PSYCHIC FIRST AID!

When you are working with trance and possession it is sometimes difficult to work out when someone is in need of help or whether their behaviour is a sign that the rite is *'working'*. Your rites will almost certainly include an element of experimentation and for this reason the fine line between what is supposed to happen, what wasn't planned but is useful and helpful anyway, and what is causing a ritual to move towards something that could be at worst dangerous and at least unhelpful, won't always be clear. This is where experience really counts because if you have witnessed similar occurrences before (when someone else was in charge of the welfare of the participants) then you will have more of an idea about what to do. I can't stress this enough.

The first lesson of psychic first aid is medical information. Ask your participants to tell you if they have any medical conditions that could cause them to faint, fit, or pass out, and what they need you to do for them in that instance. The second lesson is whether they have had any past instances where they have lost control of their trance state and needed help from someone else. Think about the abilities you personally and your ritual team have in dealing with such instances if they were to arise again. This is not to say that you should automatically exclude people, far from it. But you should have an action plan agreed with this kind of participant that you will put into place if a similar thing occurs.

I would strongly advise that you plan your rite so that only a certain percentage of the participants will enter a deep trance (i.e. an underworld journey or possession). An even better idea would be to focus the energy of the ritual onto only one or two people who will enter the deeper trance state. The majority of the rest of the participants would then enter a light to medium trance over which they would continue to keep an element of control. You can then also have one or two people who are designated as watchers – they are involved in the ritual but they make sure that they keep enough control that they will notice if there are any problems and are ready to step in. Ideally, one person should be keeping watch for every person entering deep trance and one keeping watch on the rest of the participants.

How do you judge whether someone needs help? As discussed already, this may well be something that you need to decide upon quickly. The intent and flow of the ritual should always be taken into accord when deciding whether to act. Perhaps more importantly, the experience, health and abilities of the person you are thinking might need help should always be taken into account.

Things to watch out for:

- Fitting
- Losing consciousness suddenly
- Speaking in a voice that isn't their own
- Falling asleep
- Disturbing other participants
- Eyes rolling back in head
- Strong sense of fear and discomfort in participant
- Loss of feeling to some or all of the body

As discussed, which role the person who is displaying these symptoms has in the rite and the intent of the rite has to be taken into account. Someone whose role it is to prophesise, speak to spirits, or become possessed may show some or many of these symptoms and these might be essential for them to communicate with the other. In this instance, keep an eye on them, and be sure that you don't leave them in trance for longer than they are used to and can comfortably manage. If someone is in deep trance for the first time, be very careful not to leave them in deep trance for too long. Think of it like being under water, without any practice you can only manage it for so long, but with practice you build up the tolerance to stay under for a little bit longer every time.

For a participant who you are planning to have enter a light to medium trance state, my advice would be to act straight away at any of the signs given. This is partly for their safety (especially if you do not know how they react within trance), but it is also important for the flow of the ritual. If something is happening as part of a planned ritual that is going against or interrupting the flow and intent of it, you stand a very real chance of losing control of the ritual. This can be dangerous. You could be jeopardising the safety of the rest of the participants, especially those whose role it is to enter a deeper trance. To veer from the original plan and to take the energy and focus away from them could mean that they lose control and are subsequently put into a dangerous position.

The best way to bring someone out of trance is gently. Often a hand on their shoulder and calling their given name can be enough to bring someone back. Make a decision whether that person needs to follow the grounding exercises given directly after this section straight away, or whether they will be better finishing the ritual. If you do decide that they need the grounding exercises (and possibly something to eat) get someone to take them out of the ritual to do so. It might be appropriate for them to re-enter the ritual once they are more in control. My advice would be that this would be preferable as it means that everyone in the ritual grounds and winds the rite down together. If after grounding you still do not feel that someone is fully back you can ask them to tell you their name and talk about their house, their parents, what they had for lunch. Constantly remind them of their mundane life and their physical body in order to help reunite the mind with the physical body. Whether or not you believe that a journeying soul leaves the body or that the conscious mind simply takes a back seat, this technique is invaluable for helping people back to the mundane.

If you feel that someone is being overshadowed (you believe another part of their personality or consciousness is taking control, or perhaps that another entity has taken control) then this technique will also work as the natural state of the body is with the mundane every day consciousness and reminding the body of the mundane and normal gives strength to that side of the personality to help it reclaim and take back. If this technique is not working then you might need to think about using a kind of banishing to remove the overshadowing. Start gently, but firmly. Say that there is no place for them here and you would like them to leave. In the majority of cases this should be (and will be) enough. More extreme situations are highly unusual, but that doesn't mean that they do not happen, and for that reason, you need to make sure that you are prepared if you are planning to lead a group through one of these rites.

Your greatest tool is your will. By this I mean, the energy that comes from focusing your needs. If you use a Seidr knife use this. If not, similar magic tools could be any sword, athame, magical knife, or wand that you personally use to represent your will and ability to command and control the energies that you work with. You could also use your outstretched hand, palm flat. Focus your energy into the banishment of the overshadowing. Visualise that energy coming from you, through your tool (or palm), hitting your subject, and with force, knocking out the extra energy that doesn't belong. You can use a sound or a phrase or word of power at the same time to help you focus. There are lots to choose from, *'Ka'*,[49] *'So mote it be'*.[50] I prefer simplicity and use *'f*** off'* which might seem an interesting approach, but I can muster a whole lot of energy behind those words through many years of practice. It is the tone of voice, the visualisation, and the intent that makes the difference.

As discussed, it is incredibly rare for anyone to need even the above to help bring them out of trance. It is even less likely, therefore, that you will need the following techniques, but prepared is pre-armed. These techniques work on the assumption that a short, sudden shock breaks focus and disarms anything that has a hold. It also works on the assumption that the same shock is enough to shake a person back to consciousness. The first of these is a glass of cold water over the head. You most probably have these around the working space for thirsty dancers so it is easily accessible even if you hadn't prepared. The cold water is an unwelcome shock to anyone. Water is also used

---

[49] Nigel Pennick, *Secrets of East Anglian Magic.* 2004.
[50] Stewart Farrar, *What Witches Do: A Modern Coven Revealed.* 1989.

for purification[51] and blessing and is a neutralising force, good for neutralising excess energies. It also works as a deterrent. Occasionally, you will find that there are people who enjoy the attention that comes from having problems in ritual. I would suggest that you choose not to work with people like this, and that you treat any problems seriously. For all the best intentions, you can't always avoid these people, you can however make it known that the way you deal with such things is a glass of cold water over the head!

The second of these techniques is the bell. I always have a bell at easy reach within my working space, in case of emergencies and I would suggest that you do the same. Ringing a bell serves again to shock, break focus, and bring someone back to reality quickly. Through folklore, the ringing of bells to shock or scare demons and devils has been recorded. For example, there are suggestions that this is what church bells were used for.[52] It is also a practice used within Indian temples.[53]

As well as this, the bell is good for purifying and clearing excess energy from a working space.

GROUNDING TECHNIQUES

Whatever role a participant plays in a high energy rite, it is important that they know how to ground. Part of leading a rite is making sure that you encourage and help people to ground at the end of it. Like the other areas of trance we have spoken about, the best way for you personally to ground will be unique to you, but there are a few techniques that you can work with.

The first and easiest is to remove the extra energy from you. This can be done by using it (shouting, clapping, stamping), but also by letting it drain out of you and into the earth. Put your hands flat on the floor (you can also put your forehead to the ground – it works for sportspeople!) and visualise the extra energy leaving your body and going into the earth where it can be neutralised and therefore ready to reuse. If you are with someone that

---

51 d'Este, *Towards the Wiccan Circle*. 2008.

52 Leach, *Funk and Wagnall's Standard Dictionary of Folklore, Mythology and Legend*. 1975.

53 Crooke, *Introduction to the Popular Religion and Folklore of Northern India*. 2007.

you sense is having trouble grounding, you can take their hands and let the excess energy drain through you and into the ground. Ideally, you want everyone grounding themselves as only an individual knows what energy they need to keep and what they need to drain. Eating something filling and stodgy is another great way to ground, putting heavy food in your body and making it focus on something mundane (you can also see this as using the extra energy to digest). Electricity (for example putting lights and televisions on) is another good way to clear energy from a space. Once you have grounded, make sure you repair and strengthen any part of your personal protection/aura that needs it.

CHAPTER ONE

THE VOLVA

Volva is a term used within the *Sagas* and *Eddas* describing a woman that worked seidr, witchcraft, or sorcery.[54] Many of the sources refer to the Volva as working magical acts, but others speak of the Volva as a prophetess. Jan Fries describes Volva as a *'priestess'*,[55] and it is clear, when you look at the descriptions of Volvas why this is. There is, in the Norse, another term used for priestess – gydia – and this is terminology that has been applied to Freyja (see chapter seven). There are also, however, terms given to prophetess (spakona, seidkona). The term Volva seems to almost exclusively be used to denote women. Certainly, I have found no use within primary or even secondary evidence that gives a man the title of Volva. The historian Hermann Palsson gives the basic meaning of the root of the word as *'cylindrical or round'* and equates it to the Latin *Volvo 'to roll, turn about'*.[56]

For our purposes, I have used the term Volva within this chapter to look at solitary seidr work and seidr focused on personal knowledge. Seeking information for one's self using one's own prophetic and journeying abilities, rather than relying on another or on group focus and energy. The source materials I have explored and discussed within this chapter are those that show the Volva working for others, but that display the nature and the energy of the seidr

---

[54] Palsson, *Voluspa: The Sybil's Prophecy.* 1996.
[55] Fries, *Seidways.* 1996.
[56] Palsson, *Voluspa: The Sybil's Prophecy.* 1996.

worker and have a core that allows the imager to be used for personal and solo workings.

THE SEER'S PROPHECY

> *"Bright one, they called her, whenever she came to houses,*
> *The seer with pleasing prophecies, she charmed them with spells;*
> *She made magic wherever she could, with magic she played with minds,*
> *She was always the favourite of wicked women."*[57]

Voluspa (translated as *The Seeress' Prophecy* by Carolyne Larrington[58]) is the first text given in the *Poetic Edda*. Its story follows a Volva who has been asked by Odin to prophesise for him. Her prophecy begins with the past, and she gives the Norse creation myth, detailing how the universe began. Her story also gives a description of a Volva Heid, who we presume represents the Volva who is speaking. She goes on to describe Odin's future and to foretell Ragnarok (the end of the God's reign and life as it was known). *Voluspa* gives us a great insight into the Norse cosmology, but it also gives us an insight into the perception and role of the Volva, as well as help devising our own Volva practice. As you can see from the stanza given at the start of this passage, the Volva's role was more than her pleasing prophesies. She could also charm with spells, and make magic. The line *'she played with minds'* gives us perhaps the most important clue to seidr that we can have, which is that seidr was very much something that used the mind to invade and change other people's perceptions of reality. *'Playing with minds'* is such an evocative imagery, and seidr that seeks to torment and *'play with'* people is discussed in more detail in chapter three.

Voluspa was written around the tenth century[59] and Helen O'Donoghue in *From Asgard to Valhalla*[60] suggests

---

57 Palsson, *Voluspa: The Sybil's Prophecy.* 1996.
58 Larrington, *The Poetic Edda.* 1999.
59 Ibid.
60 O'Donoghue, *From Asgard to Valhalla: The Remarkable History of the Norse Myths.* 2008.

recent examinations suggest that it was written before Iceland's conversion to Christianity and therefore is *"a pagan response to Christian theology."*[61] Further theories suggest that the dating of the text, as well as the subject area, means that the author would have had access to and therefore borrowed ideas from the Classical world. Certainly, there are similarities between the Volva of the Norse and the Sibyl of the Hellenic world. More information about this is found in chapter eight. As part of the *Codex Regis* texts, who wrote it is not known, and with it any ability to understand bias that the author may have had. The poet is writing in the voice of the prophetess, and the understanding they show for the Volva has led some academics to question whether the poet was in fact a female who had played the part of the Volva.[62] Was *Voluspa* written by a Volva? It is an interesting theory and a rather inspiring one for the modern day seidkona reader to think that we have in *Voluspa "the earliest female voice in Old Norse known to us"*[63] but we can't know for sure either way. The author of *Voluspa* at present remains, and is likely to remain, anonymous.

The name Heid is translated in the stanza above as *'bright one'* and within the stanza, Heid, the prophetess is telling her story. She starts her tale before this point *"as far back as it is possible to go"*[64] with the story of creation. This allows us to understand that she has access to information that forms the very existence of the universe and is beyond the capabilities of her mortal life to be in memory of. Another theory, of course, is that the prophetess is older than time and therefore is seen by Odin and by mankind as immortal, ever present and ever knowing.

The name Heid is a common name used by sibyls and sorceresses throughout the literature available. Many different *Sagas* that feature a Volva call her Heid. Examples of this can be found in *Landnamabok, Fridhjolf's Saga, Fraekna,* and *Hrolf Kraki's Saga* to name a few.[65] There are too many instances of Volvas with the name Heid

---

[61] O'Donoghue, *From Asgard to Valhalla.* 2008.
[62] Palsson, *Voluspa: The Sybil's Prophecy.* 1996.
[63] Ibid.
[64] O'Donoghue, *From Asgard to Valhalla.* 2008.
[65] Chisholm & Flowers (eds), *A Source-book of Seid,* 2002.

for it to be a complete coincidence, so where does the name come from?

The first mention that we have of Heid is during the *Voluspa*, but it is clear that Heid is seen as a prophetess. Heid is often linked with Gullveig as the stanza before tells of Gullveig being burnt three times in the flames by the Aesir (Gullveig was a Vanir goddess who was visiting the Aesir gods but her gold lust was considered problematic by them. The action of burning Gullveig started the war between the Aesir and the Vanir). Gullveig has sometimes been linked with the goddess Freyja as another of her aspects.[66] Is Heid/Bright One a name used for Gullveig? If so, this assumes that Heid was not a mortal prophetess but a Vanir goddess. Did Gullveig, once put through the flames, transform into Heid whereupon she became the Volva? If the flames were transformative and effected changes in Heid, can we see them as being an initiatory experience for her that gave her the skills she needed to prophesise and work seidr?

The link between the original bright one and her namesakes is an interesting one. Was Heid the name of office given to Volvas whilst they were working, or once they had gone through their training and transformation into Volvas? Or was Heid something that the Volvas became for their seidr and prophecy work? There are examples given in the *Sagas* that show a belief in deity possession (see chapter seven), was a visit from Heid similar to a visit from Odin in that the Volva was possessed by the energy and nature of Heid when they prophesised?

As well as considering that the author of *Voluspa* might have been a Volva, Palsson also suggests that the *"ecstatic tone of Voluspa might lead to the suspicion that it was composed in an abnormal state of mind."*[67] Certainly, the poem does have an ecstatic feel to it, and this brings us to consider trance states and whether the Volvas went into trance. My first thought about whether the author of *Voluspa* wrote in an abnormal state of mind is simply that a lot of poets and writers describe their work as coming from somewhere other than their conscious mind. Some of the best known literature has an otherworldly feel to it (for example, C.S. Lewis felt that *The Chronicles of Narnia* were

---

[66] McGrath, *Asyniur.* 1997
[67] Palsson, *Voluspa.* 1996

inspired as much as composed.) The act of writing, and particularly of writing poetry can be seen to automatically put the author into an altered state of consciousness, as does any other art that involves deep concentration and subsequent creation. But is the ecstatic nature of the wording deliberate or accidental? And did Volvas go into trance whilst they prophesised?

Voluspa finishes with *"now she must sink down"*[68] which Palsson presumes could refer to the Volva sinking out of her trance state.[69] Certainly, changing between levels of consciousness can be likened to either sinking or climbing (and sometimes flying) so this is a consideration. Another theory that we could consider is that the Volva is sinking back into the grave, which links the Volva to the Norse practice of Utiseta (Utiseta was *'sitting out'*, spending the night outside, often on grave mounds,[70] in order to gain wisdom from the ancestors, see chapter five for further information). Palsson believes that the line *"alone she sat outside, when the old man came"*[71] could refer to the Volva *'sitting out'* or utiseta.

The *'old man'* of course refers to the god Odin who Heid is prophesying for.

"Why do you question me? What do you test me?"[72] she asks, *"I know everything Odin, where you hid your eye"*.[73] Palsson believes that by telling Odin that she knows where he hid his eye, she is showing her abilities, as no one else but Odin knew this.[74] By telling him things that she cannot know, she is demonstrating that the rest of her prophecy (the part that is yet to come and Odin himself is waiting to find out) is also valid. However, Odin's eye is hidden in the well of Mimir, the wise, which gives Odin access to another source of otherworldly wisdom. Why in that case, does he need to find Heid and question her? Is this what she is asking Odin? Rather than *'I know it all, here is my proof'*, she is instead asking *'why are you asking me?'*

---

68 Larrington, *The Poetic Edda*. 1999.
69 Palsson, *Voluspa*. 1996.
70 Fries, *Seidways*. 1996.
71 Larrington, *The Poetic Edda*. 1999.
72 Ibid.
73 Palsson, *Voluspa*. 1996.
74 Ibid.

Becoming The Volva

The transformation of Gullveig into Heid leads us to look at the first action in our quest to become the Volva – the initiatory transformation. This is not the only example within the *Eddas* that can be seen as initiatory or transformative. We also have the story of Freyja's favourite Ottar transforming into a boar, and the story of Mimir's wisdom after his head is cut off by the Vanir. The tale of Odin, disguised as Grimnir also gives hints of transformation and ecstatic knowledge through torture, as does Odin sacrificing himself to himself on Yggdrasil to gain the knowledge of the runes. Knowledge and wisdom it seems, within the literature of the Norse, is something that requires transformation to achieve. This theme is of course echoed in other cultures – for example Taliesin in the Welsh, and Dionysus in the Greek.

Therefore, it is not too great a leap of faith to consider the first act of becoming the Volva would be to undergo a transformative initiatory style process. Indeed, it is a theme that we see often within the modern pagan movement, and the journey based initiatory experience of the contemporary seeress Raudhildr is described by Jenny Blain[75] and Robert J Wallis.[76] This account comes from Jenny Blain's *Nine Worlds of Seid Magic*:

> "The Maurnir have much wisdom, and she asked (again, naively, she says) if they would teach her, if she could learn from them, share in their wisdom. They said no, they couldn't teach her, but if she wished she could become part of the wisdom. She agreed that this would be a good thing.
> So they ate her.
> They threw aside the bones, as they ate. Her bones were lying on the cavern floor, when Loki appeared and started dancing and singing, calling to the goddesses and gods to put her back together, which they eventually did."[77]

This was part of a trance journey (please see the introduction for more on journeys) and as such Raudhildr was experiencing the above as part of an inner world path working whilst in an altered state of consciousness.

75 Blain, *Nine Worlds of Seid-Magic*. 2001.
76 Wallis, *Shamans/Neo-Shamans*. 2003.
77 Blain, *Nine Worlds of Seid-Magic*. 2001.

Journeying is a very good way of achieving inner transformation. Although it is a good idea to state your Journey intent and to have a brief formulation of plan, the amount that you plan is up to you. Of course, you might find that the Gods have another plan for your journey and within a journey where you are specifically asking for spiritual transformation, you would be wise to work with whichever path that journey takes for you. It might be that you decide instead of a formulated plan, that you want to work specifically with a deity you work closely with and ask them to transform you into a Volva. Be sure whether you mean within inner/ outer realm journeying or you mean to have a transformative experience in real life. If you choose real life, remember that part of the Volva's role is to walk the worlds (including the underworld) and to deal with ancestors and spirits) and be prepared for something spectacular and life changing (the Norse are not known for their subtlety) If you do choose this path, good luck! The less hardcore of the two choices is likely to be an initiatory journey, but again, don't underestimate the unsubtle nature of the Norse deities and be prepared. The path of the Volva is not for the feint hearted!

Experiences you might plan to encounter within your journey, or might encounter (whatever your original 'plans') would be likely to echo the transformative and initiatory examples given within the *Sagas* and *Eddas*. The right deity to dedicate your transformation to (and therefore gain divine assistance from) will hopefully, by the time you get to transformation stage) become very clear to you. If it doesn't, do your research on the Norse gods and find some time to journey and meet with individual gods. Likely deities for your transformation would include Freyja and Odin (more about both of these gods within chapter seven). If you consider Gullveig to be an aspect of Freyja, you can see that she has undergone a transformation to become a Volva. She also transforms her favourite, Ottar, as well as being understood to have taught seidr to the Aesir. Odin has undergone his own transformative experiences, both on the world tree, and with the removal of his eye. Frigga and Hel would also be good deities to dedicate your transformation to. Frigga spins the wool that is woven into the web of wyrd, and Hel rules Helheim (see chapter seven for more information on both of these goddesses).

BECOMING THE VOLVA:

RITE OF TRANSFORMATION

> *This is a personal rite so use your experience of what works for you. Do you like to fast and purify your body before rituals? Do you like to work indoors or outdoors? Do you want to invoke any personal spirits and guides before you start? Will you put up any protection or raise energy for your rite?*
>
> *Although the rites in this book are given in a way that allows them to be picked up and used immediately in their entirety, I encourage you to not do this but to borrow themes and ideas and adapt them to suit you. After all, seidr is a path that does not come with an instruction manual, and even if it did, it would be something that someone else made up or had inspired by deity. Why should you not be responsible for your own practice?*

* **Purify the space using a transformative blend of incense** *(benzoin, amber, juniper, mugwort works well)*
* **Cast a disir circle** *(see chapter six) for protection*
* **Invoke your chosen deity** *(see chapter seven)*
* **State the intent of your journey.** *For example "With Freyja's help, and the use of smoke and flames, I will step into the fire of transformation and the Volva spirit will be awoken inside me, giving me the gifts of prophecy and sorcery. As a sacrifice for these gifts, I release my fear and ignorance." Be very clear when you state your intent, the Norse energy is very direct. Be sure, if you are asking for something from the journey (for example the gift of prophecy or the ability to travel safely into the underworlds) that you know and state what you are offering as an exchange. It doesn't have to be personal qualities, as shown in the example, it can be time, or a task, or simply a dedication to the path of the Volva.*
* **Use your incense to create a wall of smoke** *by putting the incense on the floor in front of you and adding a large amount of incense onto your charcoal. If you want it to look very dramatic (and you don't have smoke alarms) use three burners in a line.*

* **Behind the smoke wall, add flames,** *either in the form of a candle (or candles), or if you are outside (which would be my personal preference for this rite) a small fire.*

* **Create an altered state of consciousness.** *As discussed in the introduction, this is entirely personal, but my preference would be to use the drum and a repetitive rhythmic movement to start the trance process.*

* **Step through the smoke wall** *slowly and purposefully, experiencing the way the incense effects you, taking note of anything else that you feel.*

* **Sit and focus on the flame, and begin your drum journey,** *use the flame as a gateway, visualising it growing larger and larger until it is large enough for you, in your mind's eye to step through.*

* **Experience your transformation,** *either through the experiences you have designated yourself in the statement of intent (For example, being burnt in the fire and then rebuilt, or stepping into the fire three times, giving a different sacrifice and gaining a different gift in return each time), or through letting the gods and the Volva spirit lead you.*

* **Use the call back trigger** *to take you back through your journey and back into consciousness. This you will set at the beginning of your rite, the most common of these being Harner's call back beat.*[78] *Remember, that it is worth reading the texts given in the introduction before you attempt a journey like this one. Good pathworking practice is to follow the steps you took to go back to consciousness; this doesn't have to be everything that happened, but taking stages such as landscapes, and taking the same pathways.*

* **Step back through the smoke wall,** *(or step back through where the smoke wall was as it is very unlikely that you will still have billowing smoke)*

* **Thank your chosen deity and explain that the rite is over** *(sometimes modern pagans will use the term 'banish', I like to think that if I have invited something to join me that it is politer to let them know that I am finished and that the expectation is that now they can leave, rather than to 'banish'. Of course, if they are the kind of entity that is likely to cause problems, you might*

---

78 Harner, *The Way of the Shaman.* 1992.

want to banish, but my relationship with my deities is not like that. We have a working partnership where if we listen to each other, no one needs to be banished! Leaving an offering for your deity in the form of food, drink, or more incense is also a good idea.

* **Thank your disir circle and explain that the rite is over.**
* **Ground and evaluate.**

BALDR'S DREAMS

Baldr Draumr or *Baldr's Dreams* can be found in the *Poetic Edda* and describes Odin's ride to the Underworld to call up a seer from the dead in order to question her about the fate of his son Baldr.[79] This is a fate that Frigga, Odin's wife and Baldr's mother, already knows, but do not talk about.[80] Odin travels on his horse, Sleipnir who we know is a supernatural horse with eight legs who was born of the fire spirit Loki whilst he was in the shape of a Mare.[81] The beginning of the poem describes Odin as journeying to Niflheim (translated by Carolyne Larrington as Mist-Hel)[82] rather than Helheim, which is usually described as being the land of the dead. Although directly in the next stanza, he is described as approaching *"the high hall of Hel"* causing H.R. Ellis Davidson to remark that there is little or no distinction made within the poem between Niflheim and Hel.[83] Certainly, it looks as though the two are described within this poem as being the same place.

Within this poem, Odin actively calls up the Volva:

"Then Odin rode by the eastern doors,
Where he knew the seeress' grave to be;
He began to speak a corpse reviving spell for the wise woman,
Until reluctantly she rose, spoke these corpse words."[84]

---

[79] Larrington, *The Poetic Edda.* 1999.
[80] Faulkes, *Edda.* 1995.
[81] Crossley-Holland, *The Penguin Book of Norse Myths: Gods of the Vikings.* 1996.
[82] Larrington, *The Poetic Edda.* 1999.
[83] Ellis, *The Road to Hel - A Study of the Conception of the Dead in Old Norse Literature.* 1943.
[84] Larrington, *The Poetic Edda.* 1999.

The idea of the corpse reviving spell is an interesting one, and the role of the corpse is spoken about in chapter five. The Volva's corpse is roused directly from the grave mound and asked by Odin to speak. It is also an interesting aside to mention here that the concept of animated corpses is likely to have been borrowed from the Classical world (see chapter eight).

Baldr's Dreams is a relatively short text, but what it gives us is clear information about the practice of asking questions of the dead. The question of course is whether the dead become wiser in death, or if the Volva he has chosen to call up was a particularly powerful one and this is why he has chosen to wake her rather than to ask a living Volva. Certainly, the Siberian shamans believed that a shaman could become even more powerful and able once they had died[85] therefore it isn't too great a leap to consider that the Volvas might have been considered in the same way.

The Volva is unhappy about being awoken from her sleep, but answers the questions put to her, finishing each stanza with *"reluctantly I told you, now I'll be silent"*[86] as opposed to the *"do you understand yet, or what more?"*[87] that the Volva finishes each section within the *Voluspa*. The poem finishes with the Volva recognising that it is Odin that she has been speaking to, but then with a twist, as Odin recognises that it is not a Volva that he has been speaking to but instead *'the mother of three ogres*[88]*'* which suggests that it is in fact Loki that he has been speaking to. Had he been speaking to Loki all along, or did the Volva become Loki later into the poem? Was the corpse reanimated with Loki's essence or did Loki borrow the corpse towards the end of the Volva's speech in order to speak his own words to Odin? It is easy to read the poem both ways, but it is important to remember that our knowledge of the deities often using a seidr high seat rite to speak to through the Seer to their audience (see chapter four) is likely to add bias to the way in which we interpret the poem today. Either way, Palsson reminds us that *"The sibyl knows where the ends of Baldr's threads are located,*

---

85 Hutton, *Shamans: Siberian Spirituality and the Western Imagination.* 2007.
86 Larrington, *The Poetic Edda.* 1999.
87 Ibid.
88 Ibid.

and by measuring them she can find out the length of his life span[89] which tells us that whoever was speaking, Odin was able to get the information that he needed.

Although, *Baldr's Dreams* is short and the description of Odin's journey to the underworld is brief, we have been given several pieces of information to help when working seidr. The first is that Odin rode to Helheim using a horse that was supernatural. This is echoed within Brunhild's journey to the underworld.[90] Does his ability to journey around the underworlds depend on his horse not being mortal? We also notice that although Odin rides towards the east gates of Hel, he does not enter Hel's hall. Is this because he is unable to or he does not need to? Odin instead finds the Volva's grave and reanimates the corpse in order to gain his information. We are also able to understand a little about the route they follow. Helheim is situated downwards and northwards.[91] A dog with a bloodstained breast (Garm) meets Odin and barks warning at him as he goes past.

In *Baldr's Dreams*, the Volva's grave is not located through the gates of Helheim. This is an important distinction and leaves us to wonder whether her spirit lies within Helheim or within the grave mound? (Or both – please see chapter five for the Norse concept of the soul at death). Does the placement of the grave show that before her death she straddled the realms and therefore her final resting place is also on the boundary? Does the grave's placement outside of Helheim show that the Volva is not mortal and therefore not subject to an afterlife within Hel's halls?

THE JOURNEY TO HEL

H.R. Ellis Davidson reminds us, in *The Road to Hel* that *"the idea of the journey into another world is a familiar one"*[92] and that other worldly journey being made to the land of the dead is a common theme within the Nordic texts. In *Gylfaginning*, the hero Hermodr journeys to Helheim. This is perhaps the most useful of the

---

[89] Palsson, *Voluspa*. 1996.
[90] Larrington, *The Poetic Edda*. 1999.
[91] Ellis, *The Road to Hel*. 1943.
[92] Ibid.

descriptions of Helheim[93] (although perhaps considered as one of the least well known.) Hermodr rides Odin's supernatural horse Sleipnir down to Helheim, and we are told that for nine nights he rides over *"dark and deep valleys"*[94] where he can see nothing at all, until he reaches a river. H.R. Ellis Davidson tells us that within this text, *"there is no doubt about the destination"*[95] and we are not left wondering about the links between Niflheim and Helheim. On reaching the gates of Helheim, Hermodr passes over the gates which take the form of a wall of cold flames by leaping over on the back of Odin's horse. Again, we wonder whether the presence of Sleipnir means that Hermodr is allowed entry to the supernatural realm and whether he would be given a safe passage without the assistance of Odin's eight legged horse.

Another journey to Hel to note can be found within *Saxo Grammaticus.*[96] These journeys to Hel are iconic and form an important part in the rites of Hrafnar.[97] Within the High Seat Rite given within chapter four, you will see slightly different iconography to those found within the Hrafnar rites, but despite the differences, the rite is still very strongly using certain elements of the journeys described within the literature.

USING THE HEL IMAGERY FOR VOLVA RITES

As we can see clearly in this chapter, the land of the dead is an emotive and inspiring realm to look to visit as part of seidr work. You will see in further chapters that Helheim and even the concept of inner and outer world journeying does not necessary have to be present when working seidr, and more importantly, is very often not described as being a part of seidr workings within the *Sagas.* Therefore, not every seidr rite needs to include the underworld, and realistically, the underworld should be used when appropriate. Although, using the realm of the dead when working with spirits can be complimentary and is a natural link to make.

---

[93] Ellis, *The Road to Hel.* 1943.
[94] Ibid.
[95] Ibid.
[96] Ibid.
[97] Paxson, *The Return of the Volva.* 1993.

There are two very specific differences in the examples given in this chapter. The first is the concept of the grave mound. Odin's journey within *Baldr's Dreams* takes him to the gates of the underworld but not within. Instead of entering Helheim and speaking to many spirits, he chooses to find the grave of one in particular and call her up to prophesise. Within Hermodr's journey, he rides into Helheim himself, and within Voluspa, Heid herself prophesises.

We then have a series of ways in which we can harness the mythology for practical Volva workings. The first is to look at journeying to a grave mound and asking a Volva to prophesise for us. This wisdom would take the form of wisdom in response to questions, using a similar technique to Odin's. A second way of prophesising would be to make the journey to Helheim yourself, using elements of the iconography during your pathworking. A key element not to forget within this journey is the assistance of Sleipnir to enable you to journey into Helheim (and perhaps more importantly, back out of Helheim again). The third way would be to use the grave mound concept to 'wake' the spirits that you want to speak to. This is considered in further detail in chapter five. A fourth way would be to use the spirit of the Volva Heid to speak through you in answer to questions. This would be something that would require more than one person within the rite and is covered further in chapter two.

CALLING UP THE VOLVA RITE

> *Again, think about what works for you. This is a personal rite. If you feel that elements of it won't suit your beliefs or your needs, change and adapt them.*

* **Purify the space** *using an incense appropriate to astral travel and invoking (a simple, frankincense, rosemary and sage blend works well)*
* **Invoke personal protection** *(e.g. the disir circle from chapter six)*
* **Invocation to Odin** *(see chapter seven)*
* **State the intent of your rite**, *for example "I wish to wake Heid from her sleep and ask her to use her gift of prophecy to give me answers to my questions. In return for her awakening and wisdom, I give this offering." Again, don't expect to get anything from the Norse entities without offering something in return. If you don't offer, don't be surprised to find that they take. Offerings can be in the form of food, drink, incense, time, or a task.*
* **Invocation to Heid**, *this should be evocative, using appropriate imagery, for example from Voluspa. An invocation can be freestyle or written. If you are planning to pre write your invocation, using the lyrical style of the Eddas would work well.*
* **Wake the Volva** *by banging on the ground with your staff. My personal preference again, would be to conduct this rite outside.*
* **Create an altered state of consciousness.** *Using the drum and incense to start journeying would be my personal preference for this*
* **Use Vardlokkurs to entice the Volva into speaking.** *(See chapter four for examples of Vardlokkurs), my personal preference would be using a wordless chant with a haunting melody, accompanied by yoiking. Continue this until you feel the Volva's presence. This you will probably see as a change of feeling within your work space. If you are using the drum and Vardlokkurs to journey at this point, you might visualise the Volva appearing in your mind's eye.*
* **Use the drum and a journey to speak to the Volva.** *This is probably easiest as part of a meditative pathworking, visualising in your mind's eye, but*

sometimes I find that using the drum and speaking the questions mean that the answers simply formulate within my mind whilst my eyes are open and I am in the landscape. Of course, this is much easier to achieve outside.

* **An alternative to the above two instructions** *is to use the drum to journey down through the earth and use imagery from Baldr's Dreams to journey to the Volva's grave mound outside the gates of Helheim and call her up from there.*

* **Once you have got your answers,** *give the Volva the offering or reiterate the offering if it is something you are planning to do.*

* **Thank the Volva for her time** *and explain that the rite is finished and she is free to go back to sleep.*

* **Thank Odin and explain that the rite is over.**

* **Thank your protection and explain that the rite is over.**

* **Ground and evaluate** *making note of any answers given that you want to remember.*

VOLVA JOURNEY RITE

Before you start your rite, read examples of the journey to Helheim and decide which parts resonate with you. Your journey needs to work for you so use the following rite as a guide, adding imagery that evokes Hel's hall and its gates for you, and taking out any imagery or steps that you don't feel will work for you. Remember, there is nothing to stop you taking this rite and changing it to a journey to Asgard (the hall of the Aesir gods, see chapter seven), or even ask the ancestors to gather in a space that is personal to you.

* **Purify your working space** *(again, incense of frankincense, sage, and rosemary works well). This rite is focused on the journey, so indoors is just as appropriate as outdoors and often warmer.*
* **Invoke your disir** *and ask them to ride with you. Although the disir circle is useful for this rite, your safe journey is the important factor so ask them to accompany you through the realms. Use any other personal protection that you feel is relevant.*
* **Invocation to Odin** *to ask to borrow Sleipnir*
* **Invocation to Sleipnir**
* **Invocation to Hel** *to ask to enter her realm (see chapter seven)*
* **Invocation to the ancestors** *(or those you wish to speak to in Helheim). This part can be done using Vardlokkurs (see chapter four). Invite them to join you on your journey to Helheim so that you can communicate with them.*
* **State the intent of your rite** *Remember the advice given in earlier rites, be clear and don't offer something in response to asking for anything.*
* **Create an altered state of consciousness and raise energy** *using your favoured methods. Drumming is a good method.*
* **Journey to meet Odin and borrow Sleipnir,** *what are you offering to Odin in exchange for borrowing Sleipnir? A journey to Asgard can be found in chapter seven, but you might choose to meet Odin elsewhere.*

* **Lead the procession to Helheim.** *As you ride Sleipnir down to and over the gates of Helheim, visualise the disir and ancestors riding with you. You may want to use a staff in the actual to represent Sleipnir as you journey.*

* **Sit on the High Seat and don the cloak and staff**, *these may appear or they may be given to you.*

* **Communicate with the ancestors.** *I have often found that the expectation within the Norse entities is for questions, therefore have one or more important questions already prepared to ask.*

* **When you feel it is time to leave, leave,** *don't hang around. Make the journey back in the same way as you made the journey into Helheim. Remember to journey back to Odin and return Sleipnir.*

* **Give offerings you promised** *to Odin, Sleipnir, and Hel. Generally, your disir don't expect offerings at every rite, it is their role to protect you, however, regular disir blots (see chapter six) are an important part of building a strong relationship with your disir. Likewise, the ancestors usually don't expect offerings, many relish the opportunity to communicate, and be fed with your energy and thoughts. Of course, you may find that your disir and ancestors expect differently, arrange with them what you need to do.*

* **Thank the ancestors and explain that the rite is over**

* **Thank Hel and explain that the rite is over**

* **Thank Odin and explain that the rite is over**

* **Thank the disir and explain that the rite is over**

* **Ground and evaluate**. *Journeys can often take on an almost dream like quality which means that the memory of them is easily forgotten or misremembered. If you want to utilise the answers given to you, it is best to write them down as soon as possible.*

CHAPTER TWO

THE SEER

This chapter looks at the practice of seidr specifically for prophesising for others. Within the literature, many of the examples of seidr, and the majority of seidr used for positive results, are prophecy based. The Volva that we met in chapter one has gained an audience. As we will see, the Seer was an integral part of the Norse community offering both wisdom and entertainment, most usually through the winter months. The need to know, and to understand fate and what is to be was not restricted only to the Norse and we can see similar practices throughout Europe in the Ancient World, from Scotland and Ireland through to Greece and Rome.

Over a thousand years later, the Seer still plays a role in society. Astrologers, Tarot Readers, and Psychics take their place, giving wisdom and entertaining in much the same way as the Seers of the past would have done. Humanity needs to grasp that which it cannot grasp, find out what it wants to know, and plan for the unknowable. Seers today display *'for entertainment purposes only'* signs, yet their scores of clients trust them and believe in their abilities. Seers today wear bright costumes and perform at corporate events and new age conferences. The Norse seers played a very similar role, travelling from farmstead to farmstead to take part in their feasts and offer entertainment, whilst dressed in their clothes of office. Prophecies given become plot devices within the *Sagas* and ultimately, they come true.

Thorbjorg's Story

> *"There was a woman there in the settlement whose name was Thorbjorg; she was a seidkona and was called the Little Volva. She had nine sisters, all of them seidkonas, but now only she was left alive. It was Thorbjorg's practice of a winter to attend feasts, and those men in particular invited her to their homes who were curious to know their fate, or the season's prospects.... A good reception was prepared for her, as was the custom when a woman of this kind should be received. A high seat was ready made for her, and a cushion laid down, in which there must be hen's feathers."*[98]

In the *Greenland Saga*, Thorbjorg is a travelling seer (*seidkona* is the term used in the saga). In the winter time she travels from farmstead to farmstead prophesising for her hosts.

The night that she arrives, Thorbjorg is fed a heart from every kind of animal present on the farmstead. This is a part of her preparation for the prophesising she will do the next night. Thorbjorg sits on a *'high seat'*, a tall chair on a raised platform that allows her to see far across the landscape and raises her above the congregation. She holds a staff and wears a blue cloak. Thorbjorg is going to speak to the spirits in order to gain the answer to the questions that the farmstead seeks. However, in order to attract the spirits to talk to her, she needs to use a vardlokkur (spirit temper/spirit attractor) which is a song sung to attract and entice the spirits to come forward and communicate.[99]

Thorbjorg asks the people gathered on the farmstead if any of them know any vardlokkurs. One woman, who we are told is now Christian says that she does, they were taught to her by her foster mother who was from Lapland. To start with she is hesitant but Thorbjorg encourages her to sing her song and is pleased with the result

> *"many spirits had been drawn there now who thought it lovely to lend ear, the chant had been so admirably delivered – spirits who before had wished*

[98] Jones, *Erik the Red and Other Icelandic Sagas.* 1961.
[99] Ibid.

to keep their distance from us and give us no hearing."[100]

Whether Thorbjorg sees and hears the spirits that are gathering, we can only guess. If she doesn't see and hear, we again, are left to guess how she communicates with the spirits. We also do not know whether only Thorbjorg can communicate with the gathered spirits, or whether the nine women who accompany her can also, or whether the congregation (once the spirits are summoned) can also interact with them? We are also left wondering what allows Thorbjorg to interact with the spirits. Is she clairvoyant/ clairaudient (able to see/hear the supernatural) naturally? Does the platform, her outfit, her staff, or her other preparations give her these abilities?

The description given within the *Greenland Saga* is the most complete description of a Seer at work that we have. The majority of the *Sagas* focus on the prophecy itself (as in, what words were given and how it came to pass) rather than on the methods used for gaining that prophecy. In the *Greenland Saga* we have a series of things shown to us. We know that she wears a blue cloak, catskin gloves, and calfskin shoes and that she carries a bag of charms.[101] We also know that she has a group of nine women who travel with her and that she needs the spirit attracting songs sung in order to draw the spirits near so that she can communicate with them. We are also told that she ate the heart of one of every animal[102] found on the farmstead and that she needed to sleep overnight at the farmstead before giving her prophecy the day after.

We can never be certain, reading this description as an outsider; what parts of the ritual were important for prophesy and the magic, and which parts added to the drama. Certainly, Thorbjorg sets a glamorous and enchanting scene and this no doubt adds to the audience's trust and belief in her abilities. We are left wondering what parts of the performance preparation are key to the ritual and which parts are glamour. For example, Thorbjorg's outfit is described in exquisite detail, from the colour of her gloves and cloak right through to the decoration on her staff. What is the author telling us? Were the cat skin

---

[100] Jones, *Erik the Red and Other Icelandic Sagas.* 1961.
[101] Ibid.
[102] Ibid.

gloves linked to her worship of Freyja, or is this something that we are assuming from the knowledge we have about the goddess? Was the material, cat skin expensive and a sign of richness or was it a sign of poverty? Is the colour blue significant and if so, what did it portray about a person?

We can assume that the important factors are the vardlokkur (spirit attractor), the high seat, the staff, and the contact she has with the spirits. Detail is given also to her preparations on the preceding night and to her attire, which we can also presume is important. Of course, her reasons for eating the heart of one of every animal might just be to show her great importance at the feast and that she was well looked after. Yet, instinctively, it feels as though the hearts are a clue to how she prophesised. Was it similar to the vitamin A overdose Robert J Wallis talks about when he describes how the Irish seers might have gone into trance?[103] A deficiency in vitamin A stops you from being able to see in the dark, but it is more likely to be found in high quantities in liver rather than heart. Was she able to gain energy that she used to prophesise from eating the hearts (see chapter nine for a full break down of energy raising and using within seidr). Another theory could be that she gained knowledge of that particular land by eating produce from it. Following on from this, did she gain the ability to communicate with the spirits of the animals whose hearts she ate and in order to communicate and gain understanding of all kinds of spirit on the farmstead, she needed to eat one of each kind of animal? These can only be speculations, the small amount of information we have will never be enough to form a definitive theory.

Thorbjorg's story remains an inspiring and informative text for those who wish to reconstruct the seidr of the Norse people. This particular text can be said to have more in common with the contemporary spiritualist movement and platform mediums than it does with the shamanistic practices that are commonly referred to as seidr today. Have we found, in Thorbjorg, the forerunner of the Victorian spiritualist medium?

---

[103] Wallis, *Shamans/Neo-Shamans*. 2003.

NORSE SEERS

Although Thorbjorg's story is the most complete, the Norse *Sagas* are full of Seers prophesising and offering their service to the wider community.[104] Jenny Jochens tells us that *"the sibyl's role persisted into Christian times"*[105] and we can see that much of the structure of the prophesising was formulaic and featured things in common with Thorbjorg's story. The Seidhjallr, or platform, that the Seers used within their prophesising is a common theme.[106]

The Seidhjallr, as we saw in the introduction, is a feature that ties many widely varying examples of seidr together and we will look into its role and importance within chapter four. Another similarity that we have already mentioned in chapter one, is that the name Heid is well used by Seers with many accounts including *Voluspa, Landnamabok, Hrolf Kraki's Saga,* and *Arrow-Odd's Saga* all featuring Seers with the name Heid.[107]

One simple suggestion as to why all of these Seers had the same name is likely to be that the *Sagas* are all talking about the same Seer. This is not at all improbable as some of the *Sagas* describe the same events and even the same people but from different viewpoints (for example *Laxdaela Saga*[108] and *Njal's Saga*).[109] The *Sagas* were written as family histories and many feature characters (for example various Scandinavian Kings) that are figures from history. We also need to remember that the Seers were travellers and would have covered vast areas on their winter progress. The most likely suggestion is that Heid was a name taken by Seers as a term of office, based on the tradition of Heid prophesising for Odin. This suggests to us that there was more known about Heid than the small amount of information we have about her that exists. Like Thorbjorg, these Heids were attendants at feasts, prophesising for their hosts.

In *King Hrolf Kraki's Saga*, Heid prophesises for the King, and in *Landnamabok* Heid prophesises that the

---

104 Chisholm & Flowers (eds), *A Source-book of Seid,* 2002.
105 Jochens, *Old Norse Images of Women.* 1996.
106 Chisholm & Flowers (eds), *A Source-book of Seid,* 2002.
107 Ibid.
108 Magnusson et al., *Laxdaela Saga.* 1975.
109 Gylfason, *Njal's Saga.* 1998.

protagonists will settle overseas.[110]   In *Arrow-Odd's Saga*
Heid even foretells the weather. In all these texts, very little
information is given about the way that the Seer
prophesises.   But in *Vatnsdoela Saga*, the Seer
prophesising is said to prophesise both by answering
questions from the audience, but also by prophesising
without prompted questions. *Arrow-Odd's* Heid differs from
this (and from Thorbjorg) by prophesising in private,
spending the evening with her seidr and apart from the rest
of the house, and then joining them the next day to pass on
the information that she has gained the night before.[111]
This suggests that she didn't share the way that she gained
her prophecy with her hosts. Was this because she needed
solitude to work, or was it because her method wasn't
suitable to show to others because of the trance nature of
it? Or was it simply that she received her prophecies in
dreams?

However the Seers prophesised, it is clear from the
Sagas that they were very much respected and that their
prophecies on the whole were trusted, and often
demonstrated to come true later in the saga. As Palsson
explains,

> *"Sitting on a high seat and towering above her
> audience, the Volva would utter her prophecy with
> authority which was based on her exceptional
> talents and knowledge."*[112]

And it seems that the Seers were considered to be
talented and in receipt of specialist knowledge.   In
Vatnsdoela Saga, a Seer even prophesises at court to help
the court come to a judgement.[113]

SPAE

You will often hear the term Spae or Spaecraft given to
the prophesising part of Seidr – the Seer.   Jenny Blain
writes significantly about the term within *Nine Worlds of
Seid Magic*. A Spakona (or Spakuna)[114] was a truth

---

[110] Craigie, *The Oldest Icelandic Folklore*. 1893.
[111] Chisholm & Flowers (eds), *A Source-book of Seid*. 2002.
[112] Palsson, *Voluspa*. 1996.
[113] Blain, *Wights and Ancestors: Heathenism in a Living
Landscape*. 2000.
[114] Fries, *Seidways*. 1996.

speaker, a prophet, someone who *"knew unspoken things by way of knowledge."*[115] The story of *Nornagestr* links Spakonas and Volvas:

> *"At that time, volvur were travelling around the countryside. They were called spakonur and they prophesised men's fates. Therefore people gave them lodgings and prepared feasts for them and gave them gifts upon their departure."*[116]

This shows that Spae was for all intents and purposes, another term for the prophesising Volva. The use of Spa and Spae links the Norse with the British Isles and specifically Scotland, who have a tradition of Spae or Spae Women.[117] There was a significant amount of cross pollination between the Norse countries and Scotland, with some of the Islands becoming part of the Norse world. It is important to remember how close the top of Scotland is to Scandinavia, after all, one of the most popular of the Norse sagas *Orkneyingasaga* is written about the Orkney Islands at the top of Scotland.[118] In the Scottish story, *The King of Ireland's Son* by Padraic Colum, we can see the term Spae used. The Spae-Woman is described as being a local witch or wise woman who had knowledge about the people of the area. She gives the protagonist a *'girdle of truth'* in order that he can learn the truth about what he needs to know by asking people to wear this.[119] Another tale from Scotland talks about a Spae Wife:

> *"I do remember that, many years ago, there was an aged woman in Auchtertool, who was accustomed to give very oracular responses, and who averred, that she had been dead, her soul translated, and allowed to return from the other world."*[120]

This story talks about the Spae Wife going into trance and seeing pictures of the future.[121]

Some of those described in the *Sagas* as working seidr are referred to as being from the British Isles.[122] Kotkel and

---

115 Chisholm & Flowers (eds), *A Source-book of Seid.* 2002.

116 Chisholm & Flowers (eds), *A Source-book of Seid.* 2002.

117 Blain, *Nine Worlds of Seid-Magic.* 2001.

118 None, *Orkneyinga Saga: The History of the Earls of Orkney.* 2004.

119 Colum, *The King of Ireland's Son: An Irish Folk Tale.* 1986.

120 Galt, *The Spaewife: A Tale of the Scottish Chronicles, Volume I: 1.* 2008.

121 Ibid.

his family (see chapter three) are seidr workers who are described as being from the Hebrides (Islands off of the North of Scotland).

SCOTTISH AND IRISH SEERS

As we can see from the tradition of the Spae Woman, there are several examples from Scotland of Seers and prophesies of differing kinds that seem to have links back to Scandinavia. In the seventeenth century, there were stories told of *The Brahan Seer*, a prophet Coinneach Odhar.[123] There is no documentable proof that the Seer existed,[124] but certainly many, many stories have come to us through literature and oral tradition. In *The Seer of Kintail*, Elizabeth Sutherland alludes to his father being a Danish fisherman. Alexander Mackenzie gives his gift of prophecy as being a gift from a Norwegian ghost, whose dead body was washed up upon the Scottish shores and therefore his grave was on Scottish soil. Both of these things link *The Brahan Seer*'s prophetic abilities back to Scandinavia.

However, it is likely that the Scottish had their own Seer traditions, as we can see from Kotkel in *Laxdaela Saga* whose seidr skills are eluded to have come from his links to the Hebrides. J.A. MacCulloch gives an example of Highland Seership:

> *"The taghairm of the Highlanders was a survival from pagan times. The seer was usually bound in a cow's hide – the animal, it may be conjectured, having been sacrificed in earlier times. He was left in a desolate place, and while he slept spirits were supposed to inspire his dreams. Clothing in the skin of a sacrificial animal, by which the person thus clothed is brought into contact with it and hence with the divinity to which it is offered, or with the divine animal itself where the victim is so regarded, is a wide-spread custom. Hence, in this Celtic usage, contact with divinity through the hide would be expected to produce enlightenment."*[125]

---

[122] Blain, *Nine Worlds of Seid-Magic*. 2003
[123] Mackenzie, *The Prophecies of the Brahan Seer*. 1983.
[124] Sutherland, *The Seer of Kintail*. 1996.
[125] MacCulloch, *The Religion of the Ancient Celts*. 1911.

He goes on to describe similar examples of prophecy from Seers in Ireland, and also a divination technique from Ireland and the Scottish highlands which uses a sheep's shoulder blade. There was also a tradition that involved the *'bull sleep'* that involved the Seer wrapping themselves up in a bull's hide and lying down to sleep, whereby they dreamt prophetic dreams, thereby gaining the wisdom they needed.[126]

Even this draws parallels with the Norse, as we can see in a Norse folk tale, passed on through oral tradition, and written down in the last couple of centuries. It tells of a younger brother who was making his fortune in the world and was trying to sell his calfskin. He pretended that a spae-maiden was living in the calfskin and prophesising for him, telling him that the wife of the house had food and drink hidden.[127] This shows again, the links between the Spae of the Scottish and the Spakona of the Norse, but also draws up an interesting parallel with the *Greenland Saga*, remembering Thorbjorg's calfskin shoes.

These stories also remind us of the importance of sleep to prophecy. The Norse Seers took the night to prepare (and dream?) before giving their prophecies.

VELEDA

> *"they believe that there resides in women an element of holiness and a gift of prophecy; and so they do not scorn to ask their advice, or lightly disregard their replies. In the reign of the emperor Vespasian we saw Veleda long honoured by many Germans as a divinity, and even earlier they showed a similar reverence for Aurinia and a number of others – a reverence untainted by servile flattery or any pretence of turning women into goddesses."*[128]

We have a very small amount of information on the Germanic Seer Veleda. The above quote from the Roman writer Tacitus is close to what remains to us of the Seers in

---

[126] Adalsteinsson, *Under the Cloak: The Acceptance of Christianity in Iceland with Particular Reference to the Religious Attitudes Prevailing at the Time.* 1979.
[127] Dasent, *Popular Tales From the Norse.* 2008.
[128] Tacitus, *Agricola and Germania.* 2010.

Germany, although it is clear that she was not the only Germanic Seer and that another prophet, Aurinia came before her and was also honoured as a divine being. From this information we can see that the Germanic people respected the prophecy given by their Seers and would trust their replies, in a similar way to the Norse. We do not know much about the prophecies or how they were enacted, although we do know that the questions brought to Veleda were sometimes politically based.[129]

Another Latin source, *The Danish History* of Saxo Grammaticus also includes a few instances that can be linked to the practices of seidr. This is described further in chapter three.

---

[129] Jochens, *Old Norse Images of Women.* 1996.

HEID PROPHECY RITE

There are several rites given in this book that follow similar themes, all of them are examples that are designed to help your own ritual writing and practical work. They can be taken and used straight from the book, but experimentation and using your instinct is the best way to plan a ritual, so focus on what you could do differently or what you could adapt to suit your own group.

This is a group rite, focused on calling up Heid and asking Heid to prophesise for the audience. It features one Seer who acts as a channel for Heid to prophesise through. This rite works better with small groups of two to six people. For larger groups, the high seat rite given in chapter four is more appropriate. Please refer to chapter seven for more information on channels before you attempt this rite.

ROLES:

* *The Channel (this is the person who has Heid invoked into them)*
* *The Guide (this is the person who does the invoking)*
* *Master of Ceremonies (who leads the rite – the person acting as guide can also take on this requirement)*
* *The audience (who are needed to sing Vardlokkurs)*

* **Purify your space**, *this rite is designed for outside spaces, but can be used indoors if space and privacy is likely to be an issue out of doors.*
* **Invoke group protection**, *the disir circle is perfect for this. The channel might want to also put up some personal protection.*
* **Invocation to Heid** *to ask her to take an active part in the rite, the intent is given straight after this invocation to explain to Heid what is expected.*
* **State intent of ritual**, *being clear what you expect and making sure that you state boundaries and expectations of your audience, your channel, and Heid.*
* **The channel has a cloak put over their head and is given a staff**

* **The Channel pounds the ground with the staff** *in order to 'wake' the Volva, whilst*
* **The audience sings Vardlokkurs to entice Heid** *out of the earth. This should be chants that bend and coil and are haunting.*
* **The guide sings an invocation to the Volva** *in the same style, with melodies continuing from the audience. The guide visualises Heid curling up through the earth and into the channel*
* **The Master of Ceremonies welcomes Heid** *(you can add an offering of food or drink at this point, given directly to Heid through the channel) and conducts*
* **Questions from the audience to be answered by Heid.**
* *When the Master of Ceremonies feels that the rite is ended the guide*
* **Sings Heid out of the Channel and back into the ground**
* **The Channel grounds excess energy**
* **Thank Heid and explain that the rite is ended**
* **Thank your group protection and explain that the rite is ended**
* **Ground and evaluate.** *The Channel may not remember everything that they have spoken as Heid; similarly, they might not remember any of it, depending on the Channel themselves. I find that within possession rites, I remember that as soon as the rite is finished I can remember brief snatches, but that longer term sometimes the memories and the words return over the next few days. Some information isn't remembered, but this is mostly where what is given has been private between the questioner and the entity.*

CHAPTER THREE

THE SORCERESS

The contemporary notion of seidr leans closer to the prophecy and divination angle than to the other (sometimes called the darker) aspects of seidr. Whilst many modern heathens consider seidr to be more shamanic and look to the witchcraft and magical aspects,[130] the resounding first thought about seidr is often divination and the High Seat. Antiquity, however, paints a very different picture, with at least half of the descriptions of seidr showing witchcraft, sorcery, and *'mind games'*.

This chapter looks at the magical side of seidr, at harnessing and shaping energy, and astral travel. It looks at how seidr was used to cause *'psychological restlessness'*[131] and how contemporary heathens use seidr for directing energy and magical workings of different kinds.

The practical elements of this chapter are given as examples for use for the individual seidr worker but can easily be adapted for group magic, either by being worked individually by everyone in the group, or by the group raising energy for one member to use the practices.

Seidr, and magic was seen by the Norse as being a powerful tool for someone to have knowledge of.[132] It was also often considered to be foreign or exotic, with seidr often being something taught by or practiced by foreigners (usually Sami/Finnish but sometimes described as British).[133] A term used within the sorcery side of seidr

---

[130] Chisholm & Flowers (eds), *A Source-book of Seid*. 2002.
[131] Dubois, *Nordic Religions in the Viking Age*. 1999.
[132] Ibid.
[133] Blain, *Nine Worlds of Seid-Magic*. 2003.

more than the prophetic was Fjolkunnigr, which Jenny Jochens[134] translates as *"very knowledgeable"* and says was used as a term *"consistently in active magic, or sorcery, where clients prevailed on male and female magicians to manipulate the future according to their wishes."*[135]

GALINA LINDQUIST AND YGGDRASIL

In the 1990s, PhD student Galina Lindquist studied a heathen group who were reconstructing seidr rites from the information they found in the Norse literature, as well as by using knowledge they had about modern pagan and shamanistic practice. Lindquist's studies formed her doctorate *Shamanic Performance on the Urban Scene.*[136] The group she studied, Yggdrasil, had been together for some years before Lindquist met them and they shared with her their experiences within shamanic and seidr experimentation.

> *"During the first seven years of existence of Yggdrasil in its more private form, as a small group of friends around Michael Gejel, the word seid had only a vague meaning, the Nordic approximation of a shamanic séance."*[137]

As the group began to research more and more about seidr, they found that:

> *"the material had a sufficiently thick ethnographic fabric to provide a basis for the neo-shamans in creating a new ritual, while at the same time leaving ample room for fantasy and improvisation."*[138]

To start with, their rites were very ecstatic and very often took place out of doors in woodlands.[139] There would be lots of drumming and dancing and ecstatic trance with wild howls and screams. Later, they focused on monotonous singing and drumming and looks at the role that seidr was going to take within their practice. Yggdrasil member Marie, talking to Lindquist, says

---

[134] Jochens, *Old Norse Images of Women.* 1999.
[135] Ibid.
[136] Lindquist, *Shamanic Performances on the Urban Scene.* 1997.
[137] Ibid.
[138] Ibid.
[139] Ibid.

"we started to think about what we should use it for. We decided that we should send the Power to various projects: people in war and famine, endangered animals, the environment and such things."[140]

They then began to use the energy that they rose during their rites for magical workings and projects, and formulated a practice that directed and used this energy within their seidr rite. Whilst the group raised the energy, the designated Volva (whose role it was to journey) would be in the middle of the rest of the group, elevated onto a chair or platform that would be covered with something like a sheepskin. This was their seidhjallr (or seidr platform). They would sit with their staff between their legs as though riding it[141] and their eyes covered with a hood.[142] They would then use the Vardlokkurs chanted by the group to go on a shamanic journey and as part of this journey direct the energy raised by the group into the project. The form that their journey took would then decide the form that the Volva chose to direct the energy. The Volva displayed to the group that they had finished their journey by raising their staff horizontally.[143]

The Vardlokkurs in this instance helped to lure the soul away from the body and help it to journey. In this way the vardlokkurs *'spirit attracting'* song attracted and summoned the spirit from the body and helped the Volva to enter an altered state of consciousness, rather than call up a gathering of entities to impart their wisdom.[144]

Yggdrasil later went on to use the seidr for divination purposes. Lindquist also talks about a kind of *'counselling'* seidr which involved more in-depth and personal questions from the audience members.[145] Lindquist describes the power (or instrumental seidr) as being different to the divination and counselling seidr. She also talks about a research seidr.[146]

With both of these, the person journeying (referred to as the volva) would be available to answer questions from

---

[140] Lindquist, *Shamanic Performances on the Urban Scene*. 1997.
[141] Blain, *Nine Worlds of Seid-Magic*. 2003
[142] Lindquist, *Shamanic Performances on the Urban Scene*. 1997
[143] Ibid.
[144] Ibid.
[145] Ibid.
[146] Ibid.

the rest of the group. Lindquist describes these questions as being more like counselling rather than fortune telling as the questions themselves tended to relate to decisions and to the present rather than to the future. The rest of the group refer to them as *'volva'* or *'great volva'*.[147] Unlike Hrafnar, Yggdrasil did not specifically journey to Helheim in order to gain the answers to the questions. There is also no specific place that the answers were thought to have come from, although Lindquist suggests that an importance is placed on the visions and the ability to see clear images to translate to the waiting group.[148]

Since Lindquist's book was published, Yggdrasil's work continued to develop and the group continued to experiment.[149] Jenny Blain writing in 2001 relayed that Annette Host of Yggdrasil said that the practices had developed further.[150] It is fair to suggest that Annette Host's practice will have developed even further since 2001 and at present she trains those who want to work seidr. Blain also commented that Yggdrasil have several Volvas who take their place on the high seat and journey individually to gain answers or direct energy.[151] When returning, they might talk about their journey, whilst still within an altered consciousness. Divination sometimes also takes place after the energy has been directed.[152]

CURSING

Any book dealing with the practice of seidr would not be complete without a section on cursing. Many of the instances of seidr within the *Sagas* deal with hostile or aggressive magic. As we have already seen, seidr was used to describe many different kinds of supernatural activity with not all of it being hostile by any means. Yet, to totally ignore a whole section of seidr practice would be wrong. Hostile seidr took the form of sorcery and worked through attacking the mind and thoughts, very often through sleep. Like many of the other kinds of seidr, a seidhjallr (platform)

---

147 Lindquist, *Shamanic Performances on the Urban Scene*. 1997.
148 Ibid.
149 Blain, *Nine Worlds of Seid-Magic*. 2001.
150 Ibid.
151 Ibid.
152 Lindquist, *Shamanic Performances on the Urban Scene*. 1997.

was used and the seidr worker would go into a kind of trance. It is this seidr that has most descriptions of male seidr associated with it.

In *Laxdaela Saga* we find Kotkel and his kin who, as part of an ongoing disagreement within the saga, are seen to work hostile seidr.

> *"Then Kotkel erected a large ritual-platform (seidhjallr) and they all climbed onto it; there they chanted potent incantations – these were magic spells. And presently a tempest rose."*[153]

This tempest then overturned the ship that his enemy (Thord) was sailing in.[154] We can see from this example the familiar seidhjallr and the singing of incantations. They then sang beautiful songs from the roof of their enemy's house in order to lull the inhabitants into a deep sleep where they would be able to control them with their magic. The patriarch of the house is shown instructing everyone to make sure that they do not fall asleep, but his favourite son is not able to hold out and falls asleep. Once asleep he is lured out of the house by the chanting and walks straight into the seidr spell where he falls down dead.[155] Sleep, it seems, allows the mind to be effected by the seidr. Sleep is a factor again in *Njal's Saga*, where we are shown a cursing where someone knows that the seidr energy has been directed at them as they begin to feel sleepy.[156]

Other instances of cursing with seidr in the *Sagas* include a step mother in *Ynglingasaga* inflicting ill luck upon her step son;[157] a man in *Njal's Saga* cursed by a seidkona so that he will never be able to find satisfaction with his bride to be. (The saga tells of him going on to marry his bride but not being able to be sexually active with her, even though he is able to with other women.)[158] In *Gongu-Hrolf's Saga* a description is given of a house with terrible sounds coming from inside it. On further inspection it is found that two seidr men were working seidr from within the house. This seidr was presumed to be including curses.[159] There are also instances within the *Sagas* of seidr

---

[153] Magnusson et al., *Laxdaela Saga*. 1975.
[154] Ibid.
[155] Ibid.
[156] Gylfason, *Njal's Saga*. 1998.
[157] Sturluson, *Heimskringla or the Lives of the Norse Kings*. 2004.
[158] Gylfason, *Njal's Saga*. 1998.
[159] Chisholm & Flowers (eds), *A Source-book of Seid*. 2002.

being used to send night mares out to people as they sleep. This is covered later in this chapter.

From the examples we can ascertain, again, that the key elements of the seidr are the seidhjallr, the mind bending aspect, and the songs and incantations. Although it is safe to assume that an altered state of consciousness was used to achieve the curses, we are not able to prove this from the texts. What we can see is that seidr was a bending and shaping of reality, helped by the dream state, which created illusion and confusion. The songs and incantations are interesting, as songs in the form of the Vardlokkurs feature heavily in chapter two with the Seer aspects of seidr. The songs for the cursing seem to take on a different form. They are given as *'chants'* and *'incantations'* which allows us to consider that they may be wordless. *Gongu-Hrolf's Saga* shows us that these chants were unpleasant to hear, which is directly opposite to the pleasing Vardlokkurs from the *Greenland Saga*. Did the chants make up the magical curse? Were the chants aimed at contacting spirits and asking them to do undertake the magic curse for the seidr workers? Either way, it is likely that these chants were harsher and more intimidating than those used in the *Greenland Saga*.

The concept of sending energy with hostile intents is examined by Dag Stromback.[160] He introduces us to the Norse concept of *hugr*. Simplified, *hugr* is someone's thoughts, and whereas these thoughts are usually fleeting and quickly forgotten, sometimes they can become something stronger. *"A flowing out of the soul could be directed and controlled by the owner, but it could also operate uncontrolled."*[161]

Instances where this becomes stronger are usually where group situations are involved (for example a church) and together the group's hugr can send that energy over to someone.[162] This can be positive or negative. Stromback goes on to say that someone with very strong hugr can find that their hugr can be sent and can be sent in the form of a curse.[163] Within the Norse there was also the concept that *avund* (envy) could also be sent as a curse, although it was

---

[160] Strömbäck et al., *Sejd*. 2000.
[161] Ibid.
[162] Ibid.
[163] Strömbäck et al., *Sejd*. 2000.

more likely that this would be sent accidently rather than deliberately, as was sometimes the case with hugr.

NIGHT MARES

Associated with sleep and cursing was the night mare, also referred to in the Norse as Kveldrida (evening rider).[164] Another term used to describe the night mare is *'night hag'* (this is used by Stromback).[165] Following on from the seidr curse, the night mare took the form of a mare sent to someone while they slept which would then be described as riding them to death.[166] There is an undercurrent in the texts that suggests that the *'riding'* was sexual. There is also the suggestion that the night mare might have been something that was sent to them to appear in their dreams rather than *'in the flesh'*. *Diplomatarium Islandicum* mentions the night mare, showing how wide ranging the belief and term was:

> "it was well known to men or women that they would enchant or work witchcraft to ride men or cattle".[167]

The night mare concept was found beyond the Viking age and can be seen to be the root of the current usage of the word, which is to describe bad dreams.[168] Perhaps we should be thankful that when we talk about nightmares we are not faced with the night mares that those in the *Sagas* knew. The night mare seems to be something that was sent by women rather than men and can either be read as them sending the night mare in the form of energy, or as themselves astral travelling in 'night mare' form into the bedroom/ dreams of their victim. We can see an example of the nightmare in Ynglingasaga a seidkona sends a nightmare to ride and murder the King of Sweden. We also see the night mare in *Eyrbyggja Saga*, where a man is found laying wounded and mutilated. It was said in the saga that he had been attacked by a Kveldrida.

---

[164] Strömbäck et al., *Sejd*. 2000.
[165] Ibid.
[166] Aswynn, *Leaves of Yggdrasil: A Synthesis of Rune Gods' Magic Feminine Mysteries Folklore*. 1988.
[167] Chisholm & Flowers (eds), *A Source-book of Seid*. 2002.
[168] Ibid.

USING SEIDR TO CURSE

As we can see, cursing was clearly an aspect that seidr was associated with during the time that the *Sagas* and *Eddas* were written. It would not be outside of the usage of the terminology to use the word seidr when describing curses. The curse is seen, contemporarily, with as much concern and contempt as it was in antiquity. Yet the concept of the curse has stood the test of time and is found in literature and cultures worldwide throughout history. Like the Seer, the Sorceress takes her place in society, offering her services to her community. Therefore, should I, as an author, turn my back on a huge element of my subject area because it has a murky reputation, even within modern pagan and heathen circles? Or should I embrace it as an aspect of seidr and give examples of how seidr can be used today to curse?

The first lesson learnt about cursing from the literature is that it is beneficial to work at night whilst people are sleeping. The dream state allows people to be more susceptible to thoughts and ideas, and as part of the role of the seidr curse seems to be *'playing with minds'*, what better time could there be to plant ideas and seeds into the mind? Looking at the role of the curse, a lot of its attraction is the ability to get the message across about how you feel and why you are not happy. The dream is a good place to get this message across. When sending dream messages, you can use the sending hugr rite at the end of this chapter. The message you send into the dream can include the words and runes that deliver the curse. Another way of using the hugr in a hostile manner would be to send it out in a night mare image, with a night mare task.

Many modern pagans will warn you about the dangers of cursing, not in terms of the recipients, but in terms of the sender. Negativity breeds negativity and a curse is likely to return on the sender. Personally, I think that any magical work undertaken in a high state of emotion has the likelihood to rebound on the perpetrator negatively, whether it was done with good or bad intentions. The reason is simple. If you undertake anything (mundane or magical) whilst in a state of high emotion, that task is likely to be conducted sloppily and without a focused thought process which is more likely to lead to mistakes. Seidr is something you do not want to enter into with a lack of focus or without proper preparation. There is also the consideration that things are often better sorted out without violence or altercation of any kind, and that if someone recognises that you have sent unwanted hugr to them they might reciprocate in a similar manner. How long do you want the disagreement to continue?

PROTECTION

The other side of cursing and night mares is of course, protection. The use of seidr for protection seems to be very often ignored within contemporary heathen and pagan circles. It is true that perhaps the protection element is not as widely written about in the *Sagas* as its more dramatic hostile counterpart, but it can be found, and also plays an important role. We can see protection as a counteraction to the seidr being worked by others, appearing in *Ynglingasaga*,[169] where the volva works seidr to block and return the seidr worked against her client. This reminds us of the cunning man within British history,[170] whose role often took the form of hunting witches and protecting others from their spells, or removing the spells the witches had already cast. We can assume that the Seidkona would have had a very similar role within Norse society.

A popular protection rite seems to be the action of protecting a hero from being harmed. In *Njal's Saga*, seidr is worked to ensure that the hero cannot be killed by any weapon other than his own.[171] *Thorsteinn's Saga, Harald War-Tooth's Saga*, and *Arrow-Odd's Saga* all describe seidr being worked in order to protect their heroes from being 'bitten' with iron.[172] In other words, seidr was used to ensure that the hero could not be hurt with iron weapons. *Arrow-Odd's Saga* describes this seidr as using Lapp (Finnish/Sami) magic,[173] whilst we are also reminded of the story of Achilleus[174] whose mother used magic to dip him into a potion that ensured that he would not be hurt by any weapon. See chapter eight for more information on Sami and Classical borrowing within the Norse literature.

---

[169] Sturluson, *Heimskringla or the Lives of the Norse Kings*. 2004
[170] Davies, *Popular Magic: Cunning-folk in English History*. 2007.
[171] Chisholm & Flowers (eds), *A Source-book of Seid*. 2002.
[172] Ibid.
[173] Ibid.
[174] Kerényi, *The Heroes of the Greeks*. 1978.

SHAPE SHIFTING

A key element of the Sorceress within seidr is that of the shape changer and astral traveller. Many of the examples of shape shifting use seidr for hostile purposes or for trickery, but there are others that don't.

> "Shape changing is a dominant feature in Old Norse magic, obviously originating in the fundamental ideas of the soul as an element capable of separation from the body already in life."[175]

It is clear from the Stromback quote above, that shape shifting was seen as the soul or a part of the soul breaking away from the body and morphing, rather than as the body itself changing shape. Whilst the soul travelled, the body would lay 'as if dead or sleeping'[176] which gives us the assumption that the seidr worker would shape shift while in a trance or altered state of consciousness. Stromback continues:

> "shape changing is obviously a more advanced art – a magic art by which a skilled person disengages his hugr in trance and transforms it into a certain shape."[177]

This links the art of shape shifting and astral journeying with the Norse concept of the *fylgia*. The *fylgia* can either be seen as a part of the person's soul or it can be seen as a protective spirit that attaches itself to the soul at birth.[178] See chapter five for more information about the fylgia.

In *Fridhjolf's Saga*, two seidkonas are paid to stop a ship by working seidr. They climb onto a seidhjallr and work their magic from there. Whilst they are on the seidhjallr, a large whale appears besides the ship during a violent storm and the whale and the storm between them create tidal waves which threaten to upturn the ship. The ship's passengers noticed two women riding on the back of the whale and attacked them. At this point the whale swims away, but the two seidkonas (seidkonur) fell off their seidhjallr and broke their backs.[179] This can be read in different ways. The first reading shows the whale as being

---

[175] Strömbäck et al., *Sejd*. 2000.
[176] Faulkes, *Edda*. 1995.
[177] Strömbäck et al., *Sejd*. 2000.
[178] Blain, *Wights and Ancestors*. 2000.
[179] Chisholm & Flowers (eds), *A Source-book of Seid*. 2002.

manipulated by the seidr of the two women which then allows their hugr or their souls to ride on its back and change its course. The other reading shows the whale as a part of the hugr of the women, with the whale shape (and possibly the storm) created by the seidkonas.

Another instance of shape changing into an animal comes from *Hrolf Kraki's Saga* where a seidkona changes into a boar:

> *"There she sat in her black tent on her seidhjallr. But things changed now as dim night follows bright day. King Hrolf's men now saw a huge boar coming out of Kind Hjorvardr's army"*[180]

As with *Fridhjolf's Saga*, it is unclear whether the seidkona created the boar using her hugr, whether her soul took the shape of the boar, or whether the boar was there already and was manipulated into action by the seidkona. Sending forth the soul/ a part of the soul in animal form is a common theme within the seidr in the literature. Another saga (*Thidrek's Saga* at Bern) describes a volva that used seidr in order to turn herself into a lion, a bear, and a dragon.[181] A similar theme can be found in the *Saga of Hakon the Good*, where a group of seidr workers *"put the intelligence of three men into the dog. He barked twice but spoke every third word."*[182] Within this example it is safer to assume that the dog already existed and was just manipulated by the seid workers. Did the three seidr workers each possess/put a part of their hugr into the dog at the same time?

In *Volsungasaga*, the heroine Signy swaps shapes with a sorceress.[183] Signy appeared as the sorceress and lived her life, and the sorceress swaps appears as Signy and lives her life. This concept follows on from that found within the *Saga of Hakon the Good* and suggests that Signy and the sorceress swapped souls in order to create this phenomenon.

Another example of shape changing can be found in the *Saga of Olaf Tryggvason* where a whole ship full of seidr men are landing to take part in a battle. One of the men, Eyvinder Kelda, creates a dark fog which stops the army

---

[180] Ibid.

[181] Ibid.

[182] Ibid.

[183] Byock, *The Saga of the Volsungs: The Norse Epic of Sigurd the Dragon Slayer*. 2004.

that is waiting for them on the shore to see the ship coming in to land. Again, we are left questioning whether this fog is Eyvinder Kelda's soul, whether it is his hugr manipulated into a fog, or whether the fog already existed, but Eyvinder Kelda manipulated it into forming around the ship and travelling with it towards the shoreline.

These descriptions of seidr can have a range of different definitions. Shape shifting is the obvious term to bring them all together, but equally, they can be described as sorcery, bringing us back to the chapter's heading. Some of them can also be described as weather magic, or as animal enchanting, or even as possession.

CREATING A HUGR-FORM RITE

> *These are a couple of examples of how you could use the inspiration of the seidr descriptions in the Sagas to manipulate energy (or hugr) and send it out in a shape to complete a task. We can see this as sending out a part of your soul, sending out hugr, or even as sending out a fylgia (see chapter five). Using terminology from British witchcraft and cunning folklore you could even use the word imp, or a more up to date version would be a thought-form. I have given the outcome of this rite the term Hugr-form designating that it is a rite that gives form to your hugr.*
>
> *This rite uses elements of folk and craft magic to fill in the gaps that the literature leave out, but it is worth remembering that there are overlapping elements which makes it a relevant area to borrow from. Like all of the rites given, this is an example that should serve to inspire your own ideas and rites. If you want to substitute imagery here for imagery that works better for you, do it.*

* **Purify your space**. *Incense, as ever is good for this, but because this is a creation rite it is important to make sure that you have as close to an energetically sterile space as is possible in order to make sure that you don't grow any little 'extras'. In this instance, I would use the runes Kenaz and Laguz, please refer to my previous book Odin's Gateways[184] for this.*

* **Invoke your personal protection**, *the intent of this rite might require more of a solid barrier of protection rather than the disir circle, use what you know and feel comfortable with.*

* **Create an altered state of consciousness**, *again, using whatever works for you. The focus here is to create a consciousness that allows you to channel and manipulate energy rather than to journey, explore, or prophesise.*

* **Visualise an energy pocket**. *An easy way to do this is to take an object that you want to put your Hugr-form*

---

[184] Gerrard, *Odin's Gateways*. 2009.

into, such as a statue or piece of crystal. Think about what you want your Hugr-form to do and what it needs to have to achieve that (i.e. eyes to spy, a mouth to deliver messages). If you don't want a physical 'house' for your Hugr-form, shape the pocket into the form you would like it to take.

*   **Visualise an umbilical cord between yourself and the energy pocket** *and Channel energy through the umbilical cord and into the shape. Good practice is to not use energy that you need for other things. Creating sound/ heat/ kinetic energy to use, or channelling energy up through the earth is far more effective than using your own life force energy.*

FROM HERE YOU HAVE SOME OPTIONS:

ONE:
*   **Give the Hugr-form specific and very limited instructions**, *for example "Go and make sure that the email I sent in anger does not get read. The email must be removed within forty eight hours and after this you will cease to exist and your energy returned to the ground to neutralise." Or "Your role is to watch over my house and make sure that nothing uninvited comes in, you will stay in the house until we cease to live there, when your energy will be returned to the ground to neutralise. You will only take energy through this rite today; it will be all that you need for your task." Be very clear with your instructions. When you are first experimenting with Hugr-forms, keep the time limit short and the tasks simple and be sure to make sure that they do not take on board any extra energy, only that which you put into them during the rite.*
*   **Visualise the umbilical cord sealing** *and the link between the two of you totally removed. Keep the Hugr-form out of your thoughts while it completes its task.*

TWO:
*   **Transfer your awareness into the Hugr-form**, *deciding how much of your awareness you want to put into it. The ideal is to split so that you are able to control and experience both the actions of the Hugr-form and your own body.*

* **Journey as the Hugr-form image** *whilst your body and the Hugr-form's holder if you have given it a physical likeness stay still.*
* **Complete the task** *that you want to complete in the likeness of the Hugr-form.*

THREE:

* **Give the Hugr-form a time limit;** *this should be as short as possible for your first experiments and even with experience the time should only be what you can totally and utterly commit to focusing for. The longer you give it, the more likelihood you have of forgetting your task and your focus and of the Hugr-form taking your energy but taking its own decisions. You do not want this. At all.*
* **Give the Hugr-form specific instructions and set aside regular intervals** *(every hour, every few hours, every day), to update those instructions. Make sure that you set your Hugr-form a specific task and that those instructions apply directly to that task.*
* **Use these intervals to channel energy into your Hugr-form** *and keep the umbilical cord attached between the two of you.*
* **On the day the time limit runs out,** *visualise the energy of the Hugr-form drawing back into you, grounding whatever you don't need, and remove all energy (hugr) from any object you were using to house.*

* **Thank your personal protection and explain that the rite is ended**
* **Ground**
* **Make sure that once the time limit is up no trace of your Hugr-form exists.** *If it does, this is where you get to banish.*

> *As you can see from these instructions, you need to make sure that you are in control of this rite and that you remain utterly focused to ensure a successful and unproblematic result. Start small, be specific, and be careful. Only attempt this one if you are completely comfortable with your abilities to do it well.*

NEO SEIDR STUDIES AND PRACTICES

As discussed in the introduction, seidr is becoming wider and better known within modern heathen and pagan circles and the term is becoming more and more widely used. With this in mind, it is certain that more people will be describing their practice as seidr. Similarly, there will be more and more discussion on what can be and what can't be described as seidr. It would be sad to see seidr becoming a catch all term in a similar way to shamanism or witchcraft, but realistically, it has a lot in common with both of these in the way that within antiquity it is difficult to come up with an absolute definition. The term shaman referred to many different people and their individual practice, and these people were from different tribes with different cultural identities, albeit from the same area of the world. This means that a definitive *'what shamans did'* was difficult to formulate. The same can be said for witchcraft, it applied to so many different practices and people and although many would have things in common, there was not set practices or beliefs that made someone a witch. It can be said; however, that both *'shaman'* and *'witch'* started out as titles that were given rather than claimed. In a similar way, seidr described many different practices by many different people and therefore very difficult to define in antiquity. If we cannot find an agreed definition within primary sources, it is impossible to expect to police definitions in modern practice.

With this in mind, I am anxious not to look to suggesting that some things are seidr and some are not, but I have sought to focus on practice that has been inspired by and reconstructed from the original texts, even though often this might be far removed from what was originally done. After all, as we have seen, there is no *'how to'* guide alongside the original descriptions. Edred Thorsson goes one step further than this and suggests that people (when studying seidr) are not looking at all the material that is available to them and are therefore picking out the examples that fit with what they already know and work with.[185] Although this is a valid point, I feel that the material in general is so wide-ranging that it is difficult to create a set procedure from it. It also needs to be remembered that this is a trap that sadly many researchers

---

[185] Thorsson, *Witchdom of the True.* 1999.

and academics fall into; deciding on a theory and looking through the information available to find evidence that backs up their theory. If this is criticism that can be levelled at academics, surely expecting private religious practice not to fall into the same traps is difficult. It is also worth considering that modern heathen and pagan groups in general are very diverse in terms of practice. Although many internet forums have great debates about who is *'doing it wrong'* and why, the truth is that even groups who are apparently all using the same book (for example Wiccan groups whose practice comes from a book of shadows) have an enormous amount of differences within their practice.

We can see that the term seidr is used by many different groups and individuals. We have already looked in detail at Yggdrasil, the group written about by Galina Lindquist. At the same time as Yggdrasil was experimenting, in another continent the group Hrafnar, led by Diana Paxson was undertaking different experiments with seidr rites. Lindquist states that the groups had no knowledge of each other in the early stages.[186] Hrafnar is described in more detail in chapter four. Within the United Kingdom several names have been linked with seidr on a more public level. Runic John, a seidr practitioner from the North of England is one. His practice is shamanic and journey based but he still works with elements that have been inspired by the literature. His journey for wisdom differs to Hrafnar's (and to ours) as he journeys to a forest and then within the forest to the house of his ancestors where he gains the wisdom to answer his audience's questions.[187] Two more names linked with seidr in the United Kingdom are that of Karen Kelly and David Scott, who Jenny Blain talks about in her 2001 book *Nine Worlds of Seid Magic*.[188] Blain describes their practice as being more focused on the ecstatic as they were used to working with people who had experience working shamanically.[189]

---

[186] Lindquist, *Shamanic Performances on the Urban Scene*. 1997.
[187] Runic John, *The Book of Seidr: The Native English and Northern European Shamanic Tradition*. 2004.
[188] Blain, *Nine Worlds of Seid-Magic*. 2001.
[189] Ibid.

JAN FRIES AND SEIDWAYS

Another of the few names that is linked intrinsically to seidr is that of Jan Fries, who wrote the book *Seidways*. Jan Fries is an occultist and ritual magician whose first book *Visual Magic* coined the phrase freestyle shamanism. Fries, whilst researching the magical and occult history of the Norse, came across seidr and associated it with a ritual technique that he had come across which involved a shaking trance. Although there *"exists no full proof that the seidmages of the old north actually shook while they tranced, prophesised, or projected glamour"*[190] the shaking trance is one that has captured the imagination of many people and become something that is associated with seidr. The shaking trance is looked at in greater detail in chapter nine. As well as the shaking trance, *Seidways* includes a multitude of information about seidr and many other similar traditions which makes it an important addition to the seidr researcher's reading list.

---

[190] Fries, *Seidways*. 1996.

CHAPTER FOUR

THE HIGH SEAT

Within modern practice a particular ritual has grown and flourished. This is often referred to as the *'high seat rite'* and is what comes to mind most often when people hear the word *'seidr'*. In chapter two we looked in detail at the Seer; at prophetesses and spakonas who travelled from homestead to homestead prophesising for their hosts. We looked at *The Greenland Sagas* and Thorbjorg's story and this is where, now, we return for this chapter. Many people today, when hearing the term seidr instantly think of the prophesising ritual that I refer to as *The High Seat Rite*. This particular kind of rite is also often referred to as *Oracular Seidr*.[191]

The High Seat itself comes from the Seidhjallr that we have seen form an integral part of many of the examples of seidr within the *Sagas*. This seidr platform or high seat has become synonymous with the seidr prophecy rite that we have spent so long practising as the Seer is literally sat on a *'high seat'* (often glamorised with some kind of regalia such as appropriate animal skins). Perhaps the most famous group practising this kind of seidr today is Hrafnar, in the United States of America, founded in the late 1980s[192] by Diana Paxson.[193] Jenny Blain in *Nine Worlds of Seid Magic* and Robert J Wallis in *Shamans/Neo Shamans* discuss Hrafnar and their work extensively. The Swedish group, Yggdrasil (who we have discussed in chapter one) were also performing similar rites.

---

191 Blain, *Nine Worlds of Seid-Magic.* 2001.
192 www.hrafnar.org
193 Paxson, *The Return of the Volva.* 1993

It is clear that this style of seidr and the seidhjallr itself has inspired many modern practitioners, many of which will have also been inspired through the work of Diana Paxson. Although the account in the *Greenland Saga* is the most complete account of seidr prophecy that survives, it still does not stand as a *'user's guide'* and therefore modern practitioners are still required to fill in the gaps. Sometimes the easiest way to *'fill in the gaps'* is to look at similar practices and borrow techniques and ideas from there. This is why modern seidr can sometimes be seen to rely heavily on shamanistic techniques, some of which will be evident from the rite I give in detail in this chapter.

DIANA PAXSON AND HRAFNAR

The group Hrafnar was established in the United States of America in 1988[194] and takes its name from the Old Norse word *hrafn* which translates as *raven*. Diana Paxson from Hrafnar has published articles in various modern pagan publications, and has shared these articles as well as the group's experiences on the internet. The Hrafnar website was one of the few sources of seidr available even as late as the 1990s when I was first researching the subject. The group focuses on the primary information found within the *Greenland Saga*, but also borrow heavily from imagery found in other *Sagas* and literature.[195] As discussed, they are most well known for their *'oracular seidr'* High Seat Rite but this is not the only Norse based ritual that they practice.

> *"The whole procedure seems to be more patterned and disciplined, less ecstatic and spontaneous, than many of the seids of the Swedish neo-shamans used to be."*[196]

The Hrafnar seidr has been described as being fairly disciplined, although it is worth remembering that the majority of times Hrafnar is being judged on their seidr is during their public rites, and the very nature of these (open, public events where the responsibility where other people's spiritual wellbeing is in their hands) would mean that a

---

[194] www.hrafnar.org
[195] Paxson, *The Return of the Volva*. 1993.
[196] Lindquist, *Shamanic Performances on the Urban Scene*. 1997.

certain level of discipline and expectation would be far more necessary.

Hrafnar has been heavily influenced by the shamanism taught by Michael Harner in *The Way of the Shaman*,[197] through Diana Paxson's attendance at various Harner based shamanic workshops.[198] Michael Harner was an anthropologist who studied shamanistic practice within the Americas[199] and used his findings to create a *'core'* shamanism that took the basic elements of the techniques, removing that which was specific to religion or culture so that he could bring a workable shamanism to the West that could be easily picked up and studied without the practitioner needing to step into and become part of an indigenous religion. Harner's influence on Paxson is clearly identifiable within Hrafnar's practice and brings a shamanistic element to the rites. The gaps in information that are left in the *Greenland Saga* are filled in with core shamanic theory which slots into the practice easily. In chapter nine I look at the similarities between modern and antiquarian seidr and shamanism. In chapter eight I look at the possibilities of the antiquarian seidr also having borrowed from shamanistic practice, specifically from the neighbouring Sami and Finnish people.

Hrafnar's oracular rite is formed around a journey to Helheim, which as we saw from chapter one, is the Norse underworld. The imagery for this journey comes from Brunhild's journey to the underworld, but also from Odin's journey to call up and question the Volva.[200] For more information on the imagery of Helheim and lyrical journeys into Hel's realms, a very good source is *The Road to Hel* by H.R. Ellis[201] (later writing as H.R. Ellis Davidson). Beforehand, the space is purified by smudging with incense. The rite then starts with energy raising in the form of appropriate music, or drumming and clapping. A pathworking is then given to all participants. Hrafnar perform the oracular seidr rite in both closed and open groups, sometimes at public events,[202] therefore the

---

197 Harner, *The Way of the Shaman*. 1992.
198 Wallis, *Shamans/Neo-Shamans*. 2003.
199 Hutton, *Shamans: Siberian Spirituality & Western Imagination*. 2001.
200 Blain, *Nine Worlds of Seid-Magic*. 2001.
201 Ellis, *The Road to Hel*. 1943.
202 Wallis, *Shamans/Neo-Shamans*. 2003.

pathworking itself often serves to introduce the imagery to the audience, some of which may not have any previous exposure to Norse cosmology.[203] The pathworking's secondary purpose, Blain believes is as a *"way of inducing ecstatic trance in the seer"*[204] Everyone takes the journey to the gates, but only the seer themselves make the steps that take them through the gates and into Helheim. A chant is sung to help them pass through the gates, and Paxson explains that the feelings and atmosphere in the room change at this point.[205] Strict instructions are given to the audience not to follow the pathworking to its natural conclusion and go through the gates of Helheim. This part of the proceedings is only for those acting as the Seers.[206]

Depending on the size of the ritual, there is often more than one Seer. The song that helps the Seer into trance and pulls them through the gates is given by the guide.[207] Once the Seer is through and ready to begin prophesising participants will ask the Seer questions. These are answered, finishing with the words *'wilt you know more?*[208] When the seer tires, if there are further questions, a second (and sometimes even a third) seer will pass through the gates and take over. During this rite, a spirit, deity or ancestor might possess the volva and speak through them but usually the volva chooses to speak to those spirits gathered and relay the messages back to the audience themselves.[209]

Hrafnar are very active within the heathen community and as such their rites have a strong community feel to them. Possibly due to the public nature of many of their rites, Hrafnar rituals include a healthy amount of costume and drama. Care is taken to ensure as much historical accuracy in regards to costumes and props as possible.[210] During the rite Hrafnar invoke the Norns (see chapter six), as well as elder kin (for example, ancestors), and animal

---

[203] Blain, *Nine Worlds of Seid-Magic*. 2001.
[204] Ibid.
[205] Paxson, *The Return of the Volva*. 1993.
[206] Blain, *Nine Worlds of Seid-Magic*. 2001.
[207] Wallis, *Shamans/Neo-Shamans*. 2003.
[208] Blain, *Nine Worlds of Seid-Magic*. 2001.
[209] Wallis, *Shamans/Neo-Shamans*. 2003.
[210] Blain, *Nine Worlds of Seid-Magic*. 2001.

and spirit guides. They also invoke the four dwarves at the four corners of the earth and the deities Freyja and Odin.[211]

Another area that Hrafnar has been experimenting with is possession rites. More information about this can be found in chapter seven.

THE HIGH SEAT RITE, MY STYLE

During the last decade, I have spent more time working with and adapting the High Seat Rite than any of the other rites and experiences found within this book. Something about the rite called to me from the very moment that I found out about its existence. As discussed earlier, my version of the high seat rite differs slightly from others of its kind and the main reason for this is a lack of information and exposure to other systems during the early years of formulation. However, it is important for me to state that it borrows heavily from the work of Diana Paxson and Hrafnar and that without the existence of the *Return of the Volva* article[212] it might look very different indeed. Elements of the rite have also been borrowed from ideas taken from Galina Lindquist's book *Shamanic Performances on the Urban Scene*[213] within which she writes about the group Yggdrasil. Much of the rite also borrows heavily from the *Greenland Saga*[214] and other *Sagas*. Some of the formulation of the rite also borrowed from similar traditions.

Over the past five years, the rite has changed very little, although it is continually being adapted and changed as new information comes to light, or as inspired participants make inspired suggestions. A description of the rite itself appears in the essay *'The Seer'* which appeared in the anthology *Priestesses Pythonesses Sybils,* edited by Sorita D'Este.[215] The rite is designed for smaller groups (between six and twelve attendees) although I show how it can be adapted for slightly smaller or for larger groups. There are five specific roles within this rite. These are outlined in greater detail at the end of this section, but are *'the seer'* (whose role is the journeying and prophecy), the

---

211 Blain, *Nine Worlds of Seid-Magic.* 2001.
212 Paxson, *The Return of the Volva.* 1993.
213 Lindquist, *Shamanic Performances on the Urban Scene.* 1997.
214 Jones, *Erik the Red and Other Icelandic Sagas.* 1961.
215 d'Este et al., *Priestesses Pythonesses Sibyls.* 2008.

'*master of ceremony*' who runs the ritual and guides the seer, the '*watcher/s*' who make sure the audience is safe, the '*battery*' who provide the energy for the rite, and '*the chorus*' who add the vardlokkurs. Within a smaller rite the audience takes on the roles of the battery and the chorus.

A room large enough to dance in is preferable, although it could be possible to use only swaying and drumming to bring the seer and the audience into an altered state. The room is set up with an area at the front for the seer. A high seat is prepared for the seer to use during their prophesising. This high seat and area differs greatly depending on what is available at the time, but the preference is that the seer is on a seat, draped with cloth or animal skin (a sheepskin rug is perhaps the easiest to find, but reindeer hide or wolf skin has been used) that is placed onto a slightly raised surface. A staff and cloak sit next to the seat, ready to play their parts. The room is dimly lit with as few candles as are necessary to see with, and as little as possible mundane objects should be around. Ideally, if you are working indoors, you would use a room that is designated as a ritual working space, or is automatically clear, as a hall hired specifically for the purpose would be. If you are working in a living space, try and clear out or cover up as much of the mundane as you possibly can. I would suggest that any temperamental technology is removed from the room. Having lost various computers and hard drives to unexplained catastrophic crashes soon after seidr rites of differing forms, I can state that there is a reason why people say that high energy ritual and technology don't go well together. Use this information wisely!

The rite starts with a purification of the space we are working in using a smoky incense, usually made up of (among other things), Sage, Rosemary, and Frankincense. Sage is used because of its long link with purification[216] although for ease we use the European Sage not the White Sage used traditionally by American Indian traditions. Rosemary is used because of its link with death and its use in purification of the corpse[217] a theme that is found in Shakespeare's *Romeo and Juliet*. Rosemary was also used to purify and prepare corpses within the Hellenic World.

---

[216] Cunningham, *Magical Aromatherapy: The Power of Scent*. 1989.
[217] Gittings, *Death, Burial and the Individual in Early Modern England*. 1984.

84

Frankincense is used for the most simple reason of all, it smells nice and clean and fresh (counteracting the smokiness of the dried herbs), and is a resin that is inexpensive and smoulders well. You will find many different kinds of incense prepared by modern pagans for use in ritual, and many people also make a point of making their own incenses. For this rite, the incense is important as it adds a smokiness and otherworldly quality to the atmosphere within the room, but the ingredients within the incense are changeable. The importance is getting the right level of smokiness which, alongside the dim lighting, adds to the otherworldliness of the rite.

After purification of the space, the rite starts with an invocation to the disir. The disir are ancestral women spirits who the Norse believed offered their protection to individuals and families. A full explanation of the disir, as well as the disir protection invoked within this rite is given in chapter four. The disir are invoked as a group, rather than as individual entities. This means that the disir from everyone in the ritual stands together as a barrier. Using a knife specifically used for the high seat rite, one person circles the working space three times. During this circling they call up and invoke the disir to stand as a barrier to the ritual space barring entry to the rite from anything that *can cause us harm or that we are unable to deal with at this time'*.

As discussed within the introduction, the expectation is that you experiment with and find your own favoured way of protecting the space. The disir circle is one example, but it is one that has served us very well. Another purification and protection technique (this one using runes) can be found within my first book *Odin's Gateways*.[218] The most important thing to remember about protection within this rite is that it leaves the ability for those who you want to communicate with to enter the space. However, you don't want to open yourselves up completely and let anything through for the reasons discussed within the introduction. Avoid using the terminology *'negative'* and *'positive'* when invoking entities and protection from certain entities. Those terms are extremely objective and you will need to be clear and use examples of what you personally deem to be

---

[218] Gerrard, *Odin's Gateways*. 2009.

85

'negative' for your rite. Just like humans rarely rate themselves as 'negative', other entities are also unlikely to.

After the disir invocation, the deities Freyja, Odin, and Hel are invoked. Freyja is invoked for communion, sometimes her presence is keenly felt and her advice is given through the seer as part of the rite. Sometimes, her presence is less obvious to the rite, but it is polite to extend an invitation to the goddess whose role includes sorcery and witchcraft and who was said to have taught seidr to the Aesir.[219] Hel is invoked because we are journeying to Helheim, Hel's realm. By invoking Hel we are asking her permission to be making this journey, and more importantly, asking for her assistance getting there and returning back to the mundane safely. It is important to remember what we learnt in chapter one, that Helheim is different to, and bears little resemblance to the Hell of Christian cosmology, and that it is most certainly not a place of punishment. Odin is invoked because, as sky father and head of the Aesir, it is polite to include him. Odin is also very relevant as an attendee as he was said to work seidr[220] and, like Freyja, his presence is sometimes keenly felt and he too will give advice to the audience through the seer. This line given in the rite is 'three drops for Odin'. The words and their Swedish translation were given to me by Leila Wiberg; whose role within the formation of these rites is outlined in the acknowledgements.

After the invocations, the rite starts immediately with drumming and dancing. Depending on space and ability, you might want to have one solitary drummer, or give all participants drums and rattles to help them keep time and raise energy while they dance. The idea of the dancing is twofold. The first role of the dancing and drumming is to allow the participants to enter a light trance state. This heightens their interaction with the rite and therefore their enjoyment of it, but it also allows a strong group mind to be formed. The second role of the dancing and drumming is to raise energy which helps to feed the entities that wish to give wisdom, and helps the seer to journey. Within many seer and shamanic traditions the spirits need energy in order to manifest. More discussion into this concept is

---

[219] Sturluson, *Heimskringla or the Lives of the Norse Kings.* 2004.
[220] Larrington, *The Poetic Edda.* 1999.

available in chapter nine. The seer will ultimately enter a deep trance, but will move into this state in stages. The dancing and drumming will allow her to enter the same light trance as the audience, the later pathworking and the triggers of the high seat will allow her to transcend the light trance state and enter a trance state that is deep enough to allow her to journey and prophesise.

As the energy rises (or seethes and boils) the drumming quietens and the participants sit in a circle. A visualisation is given that tells the participants that the world tree Yggdrasil stands tall and strong in the centre of the circle. A spiral staircase leads down it which allows entities to journey between the worlds, and to gather in Helheim where they will meet and speak with the seer. It is made clear that the entities do not stay in the working space but that they pass through. The participants begin chanting the Vardlokkurs (spirit attracting songs) which consist of four short lines and are designed to become circular and break down as the participants lose concentration and their consciousness shifts. While the Vardlokkurs are spoken, the participants may choose to sway and clap. When the Master of Ceremony feels that the seer is ready to journey, he signals to the main drummer. At this point the drumming stops and the chanting of the Vardlokkurs quietens. The Vardlokkur will not stop until the Seer is leaving Helheim. This is in order to keep the energy levels high, but also to keep the concentration and light trance state of the participants. The high seat ritual requires high levels of focus for all concerned. If some of your participants are less experienced at keeping focus during ritual, the concentration levels needed to sustain the chant helps them to achieve this.

The Seer is helped to stand and is given an individual pathworking by the Master of Ceremony to take them down through the earth and through the gates of Helheim. This pathworking can only be heard by the Seer. The final 'push' through the gates is given to the seer as making their way through blocks of fire and ice intermittently. This pathworking is matched in the physical, in that the Guide physically pulls the Seer as they guide them astrally through the gates. The Seer is then given the staff and a necklace of Amber to keep them safe. The cloak is put on them so that the hood completely covers their face. They are then sat on the High Seat facing the audience. The Guide asks the Seer if they are ready for their first question. If they are, the Master of Ceremony begins conducting the questions from the audience, leading individuals up one by one to kneel before the Seer and ask their question. Depending on the seer themselves, questioners are often asked before the rite not to touch the seer.

The answers given by the Seer can vary widely from Seer to Seer and also from question to question. Some Seers will be given images and will describe these to the questioner in answer to their question. Some Seers will give cryptic answers; others may give clear and specific answers. Some Seers will *'see'* the entities they are speaking to and talk to them to gain the answers. Some Seers might feel that the entities are using them as a channel to speak through and give their wisdom to the questioner. Some answers are fully understandable on a mundane level, some answers are given in the form of riddles or puzzles and will take further examination, some of these not becoming clear for many years afterwards.

At the end of the rite the Seer is taken back through the pathworking and brought back to every day consciousness (being sure to follow the same steps back as they took on the journey out). All participants are given something to eat and drink and work to ground the energy within the working space as well as the excess energy they are holding. (Examples of grounding are given in the introduction). The entities are asked to return to the realms that they came from (via Yggdrasil as the gateway). Odin, Hel, and Freyja are thanked and asked to return to where they reside. (If you prefer, you can simply state to the deities that the rite is over and they are welcome to leave now if they wish). The disir are thanked and the disir barrier is taken down, although the understanding is given that the disir do not leave their charges. The number of questions a Seer is able to answer depends from Seer to Seer and rite for rite. An experienced Seer will be more practiced in spending time in Helheim and will be able to stay there for longer. A Seer who is experienced in trance work but maybe not with journeying to Helheim will be physically able to stay in trance for longer than those without experience, but they will need to be watched more carefully for signs that they are getting comfortable within Helheim. An experienced Seer should know when they are tiring, or they will let their Master of Ceremony know when the visions are fading. It is important that the Master of Ceremony is also able to watch for when it is time for their Seer to leave.

ROLES AND EXPECTATIONS:

THE SEER

The Seer is clearly an important part of the High Seat Rite. It is their responsibility to take the journey down into Helheim and to communicate with the spirits gathered waiting. It is expected that they enter a deeper altered state than the rest of the participants but they still need to remain focused on the task that they have been given. In the case of the High Seat Rite, the expectation is that they journey to Helheim and answer questions put to them by the audience. Within anything like this there might need to be a slight bit of leeway and veering away from the plan. After all, you can't plan everything and if everything went exactly to script you would end up with a lovely drama, but not necessarily a living, breathing rite.

The level of trance needed for a Seer to journey and prophesise is likely to be different from Seer to Seer. For me, it is a fine line, I need to be in enough of a trance that I am dislocated from my every day consciousness, and to a certain extent dislocated also from my subconscious. Too deep a trance, however, means that you don't engage with the rite and also that it takes longer to remember what happened within the journey. Even deeper means that you then lack the ability to communicate and might risk also taking away the individual cues that you are ready to leave the underworld before it becomes too comfortable for you (more on this in a moment).

The journey to Helheim is one that is taken astrally. A part of your being travels to Helheim in order to communicate with the spirits. However, a part of your consciousness and being also stays within the room which allows you to communicate with the audience. More information on the Norse concept of the soul can be found in chapter four. The Seer must be confident working out of body, and they must be experienced within trance work and journeying. While a seer is in training it is essential to keep rites on the smaller side and the audience almost entirely of those with experience who can be trusted to focus. While the seer is in training, part of the discipline they learn is to keep to the ritual plan. The plan in the High Seat Rite is to journey to Helheim to speak to the spirits gathered, and then to come back. It might be tempting to journey elsewhere, and it might even be something that seems absolutely essential. If it is essential, agree a time to go back and do it. You are not refusing your calling, simply postponing for a more convenient time. An experienced seer will still find other elements sometimes appear in the journey for them and they need to take the decision what to do under these circumstances. If this is a large rite and lots of people have come expecting to witness a journey to Helheim, they will probably take the same routes as the seer in training. If it is a smaller, more personal rite, they might take a detour, but it is important to let the Master of Ceremony know what is happening and what you are planning before you do so.

One problem with changing tack during a High Seat Rite is that it is not only the expectations of your physical audience that you have to meet. The spirits will have gathered in anticipation of having their say on questions. If these questions have been building up over a few days, you know that the answers will be formulating in a similar way. Those answers are not going to go away quietly. If the spirits can't communicate in Helheim, where are they going to communicate with the audience members they were planning on talking to? You need to make arrangements or they will make their own.

For the High Seat Rite that we conduct, a seer needs to have an understanding of possession and spirit/ ancestor work as well as the journeying and trance experience. This is because sometimes an entity will want to bypass the conversation stage and pass their message on directly. Mostly, from my experience, it is usually deity that decides to work in this way, but sometimes ancestors will try it too. It is up to the seer to make a judgement whether or not they allow this but if they are not experienced with either possession or with refusing possession (i.e. they recognise the signs and take steps to stop it happening) they might not understand what is happening until it is too late. Mostly, I take the view that I want to pass messages on myself. Also, I am very much of the opinion that it is polite to ask permission - so if something hasn't, I'm not going to trust that they won't also respect the rest of the rules of the rite. I have, on occasion, used possession within the High

Seat Rite while I am seeing, but this is almost exclusively due to a privacy issue (it is something that is to be shared between the questioner and the entity and not to include me.) As discussed, this is something that the Seer is responsible for making the judgement on, but they need to know it is happening.

Another judgement call that usually the Seer makes is when it is time to leave Helheim. Every seer will have their own cues so it is important that they become aware of these. The Master of Ceremony will also have an idea on these cues and therefore be able to step in and bring the Seer back when they feel that it is appropriate. My cues as a seer are subtle, but I begin to feel safe and warm and very comfortable in Helheim. It feels as though it is somewhere I could be made welcome and I start thinking about sleep. Occasionally I have ignored these cues (I don't recommend this) and I then begin to feel myself getting smaller and closing in, which is a similar feeling to the one I get when I am about to faint. I haven't experimented with what happens if I ignore this second cue. Maybe one day I will, but I get the feeling that it isn't a good idea! Obviously, when you are training to be a seer, you want to react immediately to the cues. As an experienced seer, you want to make sure that you are safe, but also that you don't affect the experiences of your audience so reacting to cues immediately is also a very good idea.

The big question when you are working as the Seer is *'what do you do if it just doesn't happen for you?'* It might seem a strange question, but you can guarantee that even the most experienced Seers will have at some point got some kind of performance anxiety. A big criticism thrown at public psychics and mediums is that they sometimes *'make it up'*. You can see the temptation when a TV camera/ theatre audience is facing you expectantly. You can also see how it would be very difficult to *'perform'* under these circumstances. As a Seer, difficulties you might find would be either not being able to go into an altered state on that occasion, or finding that the pathway to Helheim is blocked for you. Another thing could be that you don't get the right level of information or that for a particular question, no one is waiting. The best thing to do in any of these circumstances is to be honest. There is absolutely no point in pretending, and besides, you'll find it incredibly difficult to fake convincingly.

A good High Seat Rite will have someone ready and prepared to take over if they need to. I have never known this to happen, but you never know, if it does you know it will be the time you haven't prepared it. If you are finding the trance or the journey difficult, pass the staff onto your second and enjoy the rite from the sidelines. If you get to Helheim and you find that there is nothing there to answer, you should start asking questions as to why this is. Remember that seers all experience differently. Chapter nine discusses the information given within the High Seat and other seidr prophecy work. Not everyone will communicate face to face with entities. In fact, the majority of people I work with as Seers will be given imagery and will interpret this for their questioner. If you ask the first question *'why can't I see anything?'* and you get the imagery coming through (based on the answers the imagery is giving you), you will probably find that you will get blankness until the question is asked, and then the answers will appear.

THE MASTER OF CEREMONY

The Master of Ceremony is responsible for the entire rite. They direct and manage the audience as well as the ritual team, and make sure that everything goes according to plan. They take the decisions on when to harness and slow the active stage of energy raising, as well as the decision of when the Seer is ready to make the journey into Helheim. The responsibility of the guided pathworking into Helheim also falls to them, as well as the decision of when to bring the Seer out of Helheim and the responsibility of bringing them safely back into their everyday consciousness. Although the health and safety of the audience falls mostly onto the watchers, the Master of Ceremony must continue to be aware of the watchers and make sure that they are in control of any situation that might occur. Clearly, the Master of Ceremony needs to be a focused and experienced individual. The best way to gain this experience is by doing and the least traumatic way for a Master of Ceremony to *'do'* is to be present at many, many seidr rites and therefore learn from the experiences (and mistakes) of others.

I would also suggest that in order to understand the role of guiding the Seer into Helheim (and back out again) and recognising the subtle hints of when a Seer is ready to go into trance, a Master of Ceremony would ideally have taken on the Seer role in the past. However, it could be argued that the two roles require very different skills and abilities so this might not necessarily be the case.

If the experience of other people's seidr rites and/ or the experience of being the Seer is not available, I would suggest that starting small and with people that you know and trust ritually is essential. I would also suggest that if you don't have significant ritual and personal trance experience you seek to gain this before you start. Lack of experience within a Master of Ceremony, however, does not automatically mean that the rite will be less effective or unsafe, just as a highly experienced Master of Ceremony won't ensure an effective and *'safe'* rite. In general, gaining more experience before you start will usually make things easier and more organised and therefore is likely to heighten the experience and ensure that things will run more smoothly. My first experience of leading a Seer down to Helheim was when I had less than a year's ritual experience and took place with very little planning in a University bedroom! Of course, this is not something that ten years later I would recommend, but it wouldn't be the only thing I did in my teenage years that I now wouldn't recommend!

THE WATCHER

For every person in a rite that you have taking a role that requires them to go into a deep altered state (especially those that involve them to take an active part in proceedings) you need to have at least one person who keeps a step removed so that they can keep an eye on them. This is where the Watchers come in. You also need a Watcher who specifically keeps an eye on the audience. For larger audiences you might want to think about something like a Watcher for every ten people. A good long term Watcher is hard to find because the majority of people attending a Seer rite want to get involved and immerse themselves in it. You can still enjoy a rite while playing the part of a Watcher, but you always have to be on the alert and some people find it difficult to stay on alert and to enter enough of an altered state to get all that they need to out of the rite.

For this reason, it is best to see your Watchers as a rolling position to make sure that everyone gets to experience and immerse. If you have a group of people that you are working regularly with you can use the Watcher as a training position. Anyone who has ambitions on being the Seer or the Master of Ceremony in a future rite can take a few turns at Watcher.

As a Watcher you need to tune in to your ward. A Seer's Watcher is totally focused on them and makes sure they know the way they behave in ritual enough to understand what is normal and ok for them, and when to intervene. Ideally, you should never have to intervene and realistically, the need to hardly ever occurs, therefore a nervous Watcher is more of a liability sometimes than one that lets the events take their course.

An audience Watcher keeps one eye on proceedings and is ready to intervene when they need to. All Watchers also keeps their eyes on each other so that they can communicate if there is an issue. The times when it is appropriate to step in are outlined in the introduction. Discretion is key, issues should be dealt with quickly and appropriately. Firstly, check that there really is an issue. Again, these are very, very rare so make sure your Watcher isn't too nervous and steps in when they don't need to. To check that there is an issue, quietly take the person you are concerned about aside and ask them. Use your intuition; you'll get your answers. If you think you do need to do some grounding, take them aside and if needs be take them physically out of the space to do it to make sure that you don't disturb the rite. If you think you might need backup, get hold of another Watcher and bring them out with you. Make sure that the Master of Ceremony is aware of what is happening.

As discussed both in the introduction and here, issues are very, very rare so it is unlikely that you will encounter any, but it is always best to be prepared (especially when you work with people who are new to you ritually).

THE BATTERY

By rights, every audience member is a part of the battery. The battery adds the energy and the focus to the rite. High energy rituals need a constant supply of energy added, within our high seat rite this is provided by the drumming and dancing that kicks it off, but also by the constant vardlokkur chant.

When you are putting on a slightly larger rite, or you are working with a high percentage of people that have never experienced a high seat rite of this kind before, it is worth adding a little extra battery to proceedings. This takes the form of a core of two to five people whose role is to 'go crazy'. They start off the rite in front of the Seer and become a part of the theatre. Their dancing is dramatic and frantic and becomes hypnotic for the audience watching. First and foremost they raise a huge amount of energy and change the feeling in the room from one of normality to one of altered states and ritual. Almost as importantly, they set the level for the rest of the audience. Their performance allows everyone else in the audience to let go and let the rite take them. A Seer rite is not the time to be worrying about what you look like or trying to keep in time and rhythm. The battery group let themselves go and this gives everyone permission to lose their inhibitions. If you are working in a small space and only a few people have room to really throw themselves into the dancing, make sure you give yourself enough theatrical batteries to raise the temperature. If you are working with a Seer who (like me) needs crazy dancing to get the best level of trance, they also become part of the battery group. Give them plenty of room.

There is definitely something to be said from having a group of people working closely with the Seer. In the *Greenland Saga*, Thorbjorg was said to have had a group of nine women who travelled with her.[221] Whilst Thorbjorg was seated on the platform, these women would form a ring around her.[222] The concept of travelling companions accompanying volvas and prophetesses also appears in other accounts. These companions could be seen as providing 'the battery', they also form a circlet of protection which 'holds and contains' the energy that is being worked with, a sort of energetic barrier. The battery could use specific chants and runes to create this energetic field. There are several examples (*Fridhjolf's Saga*, *Volsunga Saga*) within the literature of the time that show a seidr worker being disturbed whilst in trance or whilst working seidr. This results in physical damage or injury to the seidr worker. A physical barrier will stop disturbances. Dependant on your audience and your rite, this might not

---

221 Jones, *Erik the Red and Other Icelandic Sagas*. 1961.
222 Ibid.

be necessary, but certainly, travelling volvas would have wanted a barrier between themselves and their audience (their clients). The concept of damage being done when someone is disturbed from an altered state also filters through to the Victorian spiritualist mediums who also claimed that if they were touched or interrupted once they were in trance, they could be physically injured[223] and can be seen as far forward as the 1950s, with Helen Duncan, the last woman tried as a witch in the UK.[224] In considering Victorian spiritualists, however, we must keep an awareness of the many accusations of trickery and of using illusion to create their *'ghosts'*.[225] Of course, this deception in itself was likely to be a reason for keeping your audience from touching your spiritualist medium.

THE CHORUS

It is the responsibility of everyone present within our high seat rite to keep the Vardlokkur going. It keeps everyone focused and makes sure that they are adding to the energy, rather than losing their concentration and thinking about something else. However, in the same way that there can be a theatrical element to the battery, having a chorus that specifically adds a little extra atmosphere to the rite really changes and heightens the rite. The chorus adds two distinct areas of sound: during the first stage of the energy raising (the drumming and dancing), the chorus' role is very similar to that of the theatrical battery – they set the scene of what is expected of the attendees and give people permission to let go. During the high energy raising section of the rite, people often find that the energy bubbles and needs (for the want of a better route) an escape route. Whooping, screaming, yoiking, and other short sharp energy releases are common and welcome. The chorus deliberately create these in order to allow the attendees to feel comfortable doing what feels natural to them whilst they are raising energy and beginning to enter an altered state.

---

223 Pearsall, *Table-rappers: The Victorians and the Occult.* 2004.
224 Shandler, *The Strange Case of Hellish Nell: The True Story of Helen Duncan and the Witch Trial of World War II.* 2006.
225 Pearsall, *Table-rappers.* 2004.

THE AUDIENCE

Within a small rite, your audience also become your battery and your chorus. Where you have a larger rite or where those who make up your audience might not have had much experience of High Seat Rites (yet), you are likely to find that the role of the audience can't include a large amount of energy raising or scene setting. The first role of the audience is to understand what is happening, why you are doing it, and what your expectations of them are. The expectation is that they experience the rite and that they will enter an altered state, but that they are not going to travel to Helheim or to attempt to communicate with anything whilst the rite is happening. Sometimes an audience member will pick up images/thoughts/feelings/words that help clarify the message from the seer, or they will strongly feel the presence of a spirit. This is perfectly normal and in no way disturbs the rite. Sometimes they are sensing their own disir or protective spirits, sometimes they are closely tuned into the seer and are absorbing some of their experiences. The time this becomes a problem is when the energy of the rite is focused away from the aim, or when the audience member takes a journey of their own which has the potential of becoming disruptive to the rest of the rite. Audience members should be made aware of the Watcher and their purpose and they should feel comfortable communicating any problems to them. In order to help the audience keep their focus, they are given the task of chanting the Vardlokkur during the questions.

The second role of the audience is to ask questions. Depending on the ability of the seer and the size of the rite, not everyone will have their questions answered and it is important to make this clear. If an audience member has a burning question, it is essential that they communicate this to the Master of Ceremony before the rite starts. Questions need to be considered and prepared. They should be of importance and they should be open (think who, what, why, where, when, how) rather than closed (think yes/no answers).

THE HIGH SEAT

The terminology used within our rite is *'high seat'* suggesting a tall or high up chair. This, I believe, mostly stems from the *Return of the Volva* article and Hrafnar,[226] although it is used far more widely than this. The terminology given in the *Sagas* is *'seidhjallr'* which translates as *'sorcery platform*[227] (I have used the spelling seidhjallr within the text to simplify). Once you begin to see the high seat as a sorcery platform, you begin to look at it in a slightly different way. For one thing, it doesn't have to be *'a seat'*, and perhaps the focus on seat takes away from the importance of the seidhjallr being raised. The seidhjallr appears in many of the descriptions of seidr (for example *Laxdaela Saga, Gisli Saga*),[228] and is present when the seidr is for prophecy but also for other forms of seidr too (such as shape shifting, or cursing.) In *Laxdaela Saga* a seidhjallr was erected on the top of the enemy's house.[229]

The seidhjallr in the *Sagas* is described as being something *'other'* and foreign, and seidr in general is seen in a similar way. Dag Stromback suggests that the tradition that the seidhjallr comes from a tradition that is much older.[230] This suggests one of two things, the first is that the seidhjallr and seidr traditions were, at the time the *Sagas* were written, archaic and therefore something that had nearly moved out of memory and use. This would suggest that whilst the Sami, Finns, and Siberian tribes all had their own version of shamanism, so did the Scandinavians. However, the second theory could be that seidr and the seidhjallr had come from one of the neighbouring countries that had shamanistic traditions. In *Vatnsdoela Saga* the seidkona that is described as working on the seidhjallr was referred to as being Finnish.

When we look at the seidhjallr, we also need to look at its role, both within the seidr of antiquity, and within the rites we are constructing. What role does the platform play? As discussed, seidr is not the only shamanistic tradition that has the platform. As well as the northern shamanistic tribes we have already mentioned, platforms were also used by other shamanistic tribes such as the

---

226 Paxson, *The Return of the Volva*. 1993.
227 Edred, *Witchdom of the True*. 1999
228 Chisholm & Flowers (eds), *A Source-book of Seid*. 2002.
229 Edred, *Witchdom of the True*. 1999.
230 Strömbäck et al., *Sejd*. 2000.

Mapuche tribe in South America.[231] Another seer tradition that used the raised platform was the Pythia in Ancient Greece.[232] Looking towards the more modern, we can think about the spiritualist tradition where a medium is on a stage in front of an audience and from this stage, is speaking to the spirits who have gathered within the congregation. This type of spiritualism is often referred to as *'platform mediumship'*.

One of the reasons for the platform could simply be to add the distance and separation between the seer and the audience. Yet, within the accounts of seidr where there were no audience we still see the importance of the platform. Another reason for the platform could be that it becomes a barrier between the worlds. It isn't part of the ground and the earth, it is higher, raising the seidkona into the air and towards the sky. It could be seen as the start of creating an altered state, of removing the seidr worker from the mundane world and separating them into an altered state of consciousness. Within the *Sagas* it seemed that the seidhjallr improved the ability to either prophesise or bewitch which means that it must have had a purpose and a role, if only within the past rather than within the memory of those writing about them. Perhaps the biggest clue that we have about its role comes from an Arabic text (*Ibn Fadlan's Travel-Report*) which talks about a seeress on a seidhjallr.

> *"They brought the girl to an apparatus which they had constructed similar to the framework of a gate. She placed both feet on the palms of the men and thus climbed onto this framework, and spoke her words; then they let her down."*[233]

The text goes on to say that the girl went up on the platform three times, the first time she saw her parents waving, the second she saw all her ancestors, and the third she saw paradise and *'her lord'* waiting for her.

We have to bear in mind that this text will be coloured by the beliefs and ideals of its authors (which might explain the paradise and *'my lord'* sentence), but it holds some important information. The first is that the girl was able to *'see'* once she was on the top of the platform, as though

---

231 Paxson, *The Return of the Volva*. 1993.

232 Caroline Tully et al., *Priestesses Pythonesses Sibyls*. 2008

233 Chisholm & Flowers (eds), *A Source-book of Seid*. 2002.

this became a trigger that allowed her to see. The seidhjallr itself forms a different space, it is not on the ground and therefore not of the earth – it puts the seidkona in a higher state. The second thing is that each time she climbed the seidhjallr she saw *'deeper'* into the unknown. The first time, those that had died recently; the second time she saw her ancestors/the dead that were connected to her; and the third time she saw deity.

THE CLOAK

The cloak has an important role within our high seat rite, perhaps most importantly, its role is a practical one, hiding the Seer's face and allowing them to become *'the seer'* to the audience, rather than the person they may know them as in everyday life. Cloaked in darkness, with the hood pulled directly over their face, the seer's identity is hidden. The cloak also puts another barrier between the audience and the seer. The cloak is linked closely to the modern high seat rite, through its use in the Hrafnar rites[234] and through modern heathens that practice seidr being photographed with their cloak hoods across their faces.[235] The addition of the cloak for the seer, I believe comes from the *Greenland Sagas*, in which Thorbjorg is described as *"wearing a blue cloak with straps which was set with stones right down to the hem"*.[236] Within this example, the cloak itself is not described as having any magical purpose. However, Blain identifies some references that describe the cloak in a context that might be seen as being within a more magical context. During these occasions, someone goes beneath their cloak in order to complete a task.

The most famous of these was Thorgeir, who during the Icelandic Althing, went beneath his cloak for a considerate amount of time in order to make the final decision on whether or not Iceland should be Christianised.[237] Jon Hnefill Adalsteinsson in *Under the Cloak*[238] tells us that *"it was believed that a good way of gaining hidden information and seeing what others could not*

---

234 Paxson, *The Return of the Volva*. 1993.
235 Blain, *Nine Worlds of Seid-Magic*. 2001.
236 Jones, *Erik the Red and Other Icelandic Sagas*. 1961.
237 Blain, *Nine Worlds of Seid-Magic*. 2001.
238 Adalsteinsson, *Under the Cloak*. 1979.

see was to sit and mutter into one's cloak."[239] Following on from this, is the story about the poet Bragi (who, given his place at the table of gods in *Lokasenna*[240] can be seen as deity), who *"sat in the high seat and had a stick in his hand, playing with it he murmured into his cloak, he got up, recited a verse that guessed parentage of three boys."*[241] It seems that within these two examples the cloak is playing an important part in the ability to make decisions. It is perhaps important also to note that these are both judicial decisions, which takes the role of the cloak passed that of simply being used for prophecy.

Alongside prophets and courtrooms, the *Sagas* also show another group of people sitting under their cloaks and these are Lapps.[242] It seems that either the Sami or the Finnish people were remembered by the Norse as using their cloaks in this way. The latest example that we have of this is as recent as the 19th century:

> *"There is for example the account of the Laplander who performed his deed for the archbishop of Uppsala in the middle of the 19th century in the presence of a doctor and other officials. Before he started he got all those present to promise not to touch him, disturb or awaken him, while he was motionless: 'For my soul will leave the body and I will appear to be dead. But in a short while my soul returns and then I awaken.*"[243]

This gives us another insight into the role of the cloak. As well as being a way of concentrating on the task ahead of them,[244] it could also be that those using their cloaks were using them to mask the fact that they were also using altered states of consciousness, or even astral journeying. This of course links with the widely quoted Snorri example of Odin laying as though his body was dead or sleeping whilst his soul journeyed.[245] Remembering the shape shifting examples in chapter three, you could wonder whether the cloak itself hides the fact that the body itself has gone elsewhere. Is there evidence to suggest that the

[239] Adalsteinsson, *Under the Cloak*. 1979.
[240] Larrington, *The Poetic Edda*. 1999.
[241] Adalsteinsson, *Under the Cloak*. 1979.
[242] Ibid.
[243] Ibid.
[244] Ibid.
[245] Faulkes, *Edda*. 1995.

Norse believed that the body itself could travel? If the soul is journeying, did the Norse believe that the body would then appear to be dead and therefore not a pleasant sight? A parallel of the Seer's cloak exists in the world of the Victorian spiritualist medium, who would be seated (whilst they were in trance) in a wooden chest or cupboard. This became widely known as the medium's cupboard and hid the medium from the audience, whilst also ensuring that no one touched or disturbed the medium while they were in trance. It was believed that if you touched the medium whilst they were in trace then their body would be damaged.[246] It is worth remembering, however, that it is widely believed that the cupboard also hid the tools of the trade (for example, cheesecloth and glow in the dark paint) which allowed the medium to create their illusions. Did the Norse cloak wearers hide anything under their cloaks?

Another example of cloaks within mythology is the bird cloaks that allowed transformation. Frigga and Freyja both had falcon cloaks (borrowed by Loki on one occasion) that allowed them to fly as falcons.[247] The Valkyries are described as having swan cloaks. Were these cloaks simply just to allow them to fly (remembering that Snorri was writing fictional stories about the gods) or were they hiding a cultural memory in using animal skins to journey astrally in the shape of that animal? Although I would love to believe that there was a tradition in the Norse of using skins to journey as the animal, it is a theory that holds bias based on what we know of other indigenous tribes rather than the Norse. However, the theory is an inspiring one and therefore one that is likely to be useful to us. One further explanation can be that the cloak puts the seidr worker 'between the worlds', taking them from the everyday consciousness and allowing them to enter a separate reality.

Looking at the cloak within our rites, it does a combination of these things. The most important thing, as we have discussed, is the hiding of the seer's face (and therefore the seer's everyday personality). Another thing to consider is that people in heavy trance states don't always look 'normal', and while a key part of the rite is other's interacting with them and questioning them, hiding the face

---

246 Pearsall, *Table-rappers*. 2004.
247 Crossley-Holland, *The Penguin Book of Norse Myths*. 1996.

can be a benefit. The cloak itself also becomes a trigger; the seer knows that when the cloak goes over their head, they become the seer. It masks them for the audience, but it also clarifies their otherworldly role and signifies their arrival in the Underworld. An additional benefit is that the seer is as hidden from Helheim and the spirits gathered there as they are from their audience, which gives them an element of protection from being claimed as a regular inhabitant of Hel's realm.

THE STAFF

The Greenland saga specifically mentions that Thorbjorg the seer has a staff and this is given prominence with the assumption made that this is an important part of the structure.

> *"She had a staff in her hand, with a knob on it; it was ornamented with brass and set around with stones just below the knob.*[248]

The Seer's staff is an important part of our High Seat Rite and it also has importance within similar trance prophecy rites and other seidr practices. Within the *Sagas*, the staff seems to be nearly as prominent as the seidhjallr, and its legend post-dates the seidhjallr as we can see in this antiquarian Norwegian law which states that: *"No man shall have in his house a stave or altar or witchcraft or sacrifice or anything that is known to be heathen custom"*[249] which intrinsically links the staff with witchcraft and heathenism. Palsson tells us that the term Volva might originally have referred to a woman with a staff.[250]

In *Harbard's Song*, Odin (disguised as Harbard) mentions the stick in conjunction with magic and seidr:

> *"He gave me a magic staff,*
> *And I bewitched the wits out of him"*[251]

In *Vatnsdoela Saga* the Volva owns a magic staff called Hognudr ('advantage').[252] We can see from these examples that the role of the staff seems synonymous with the ability to work magic and it is a fair assumption to make that the staff itself was what allowed the protagonists to work the magic. It is tempting to link the staff with the broomstick

---

[248] Jones, *Erik the Red and Other Icelandic Sagas.* 1963.
[249] Chisholm & Flowers (eds), *A Source-book of Seid.* 2002.
[250] Palsson, *Voluspa.* 1996.
[251] Larrington, *The Poetic Edda.* 1999.
[252] Palsson, *Voluspa.* 1996.

found so often within British stories about witchcraft as it seems to play a very similar role. It is also tempting to link the staff with the magic wand found within contemporary fantasy and fairy stories, and also occasionally within contemporary paganism and magickal orders.

Within the first chapter we looked at the Swedish group Yggdrasil and their work within Seidr. The broomstick analogy comes into its own here as the Yggdrasil seers often used their staffs to 'ride' and journey, putting the staff between their legs to ride,[253] as though riding the world tree itself. Witches within British folk stories are often pictured riding their broomsticks. The role of the broomstick within these stories is often debated, with opinions differing between it being just a handy household object, through to the broomstick representing a fertility symbol and therefore a symbol of the old fertility religion. Could we also add to the opinions with a suggestion that the broomstick is a long forgotten memory of the Volva's staff?

The world tree is another symbolism that is sometimes given for the staff. The tree Yggdrasil is used to journey between the nine worlds and the staff represents that tree. This is a concept borrowed from other Northern Shamanistic traditions, notably the Sami,[254] Finland, and Siberia.[255] Heather O'Donoghue in *From Asgard to Valhalla* tells us that:

> "the practice of shamanism among northern Siberian tribes such as the Sami involves the ascent of a tree (or stylised representation of it) to gain the wisdom of otherworld spirits; while the ritual takes place, the shaman may collapse as if unconscious or dead, while, as his followers suppose, his spirit journeys more widely."[256]

The concept of climbing a central pole to journey also appears in eastern mythology. The link between the staff and journeying is one that appears fairly regularly within contemporary seidr, but do we have any evidence to suggest that the staff allowed the volvas of antiquity to journey? Would it not make more sense, based on the evidence available, to suggest that the seidhjallr allowed the Volva to

---

[253] Lindquist, *Shamanic Performances on the Urban Scene.* 1997.
[254] Dubois, *Nordic Religions in the Viking Age.* 1999.
[255] Hutton, *Shamans.* 2007.
[256] O'Donoghue, *From Asgard to Valhalla.* 2008.

journey, the cloak masked the journeying, and that the staff (if we remember that *Harbard's Song* spoke of the staff bewitching) was used to direct and perform the seidr?

Whatever the staff was used for in the past, within our rites, I see it as a link to the world tree that allows the seer to journey between the worlds. By holding the staff they can allow their consciousness to travel, with the staff itself providing the link between the worlds. The staff also has a very practical part in the rite, firstly as a support, simply giving the seer something to lean on while in trance, and secondly for the seer to use as a form of communication to show that they have finished and are ready to return. The staff can even be used to drum on the earth (or on grave mounds) in order to wake the spirits.

HELHEIM

It will have become clear that Helheim, the realm of the dead, has a very important role within our high seat rites. As discussed in chapter one, Helheim should not be confused with the Christian concept of Hell, even though the name has been borrowed from the Norse. Hell has more in common with hot and misty, fiery Muspellheim than it does with the serene and quiet land of Helheim. Snorri also mentions halls that the wicked dead go to, Nastrandir for murderers, and Hvergelmir. Snorri, being a Christian would have had knowledge of the Christian concept of Hell and he does not link this with Helheim or even portray them similarly. It is worth remembering, at this point, that much of the imagery that we remember of the Christian Hell comes from Dante[257] and therefore Snorri's impression of Hell might have been very different. The Norse land of the dead has more in common with the Hellenic concept of the Underworld than it does with the Christian.

Helheim is ruled by the goddess Hel, although strictly speaking, originally she wasn't a goddess.[258] Please see chapter six for more information on Hel. Her realm is where those who have died from sickness or old age go after their death.[259] This really describes the majority of deaths; those that happened through natural causes. It is common knowledge within even those who haven't studied Norse

---

257 Dante, *Dante: Inferno.* 2006.
258 Faulkes, *Edda.* 1995.
259 Crossley-Holland, *The Penguin Book of Norse Myths.* 1996.

history that those who died with sword in hand would go to join Odin in Valhalla after death. However, Odin chooses only half of the battle slain, the first half are claimed by Freyja for her hall.[260] It isn't only those that die on the battlefield that are claimed by certain deities, often favourites join their patrons on death, and within *Egil's Saga* a young woman hopes to join Freyja's hall after she commits suicide.[261]

The *Greenland Saga* and the other *Sagas* that mention prophecy do not link prophesising with Helheim. As discussed in chapter one, the link with death and the underworld comes from Odin's conversations with Volvas rather than the later descriptions of prophecy. What we can see within the *Sagas*, however, seems to be a general confusion between Helheim and Niflheim, as though the two worlds are the same. We saw, in chapter one, that Odin's journey to the Underworld gives both names. We can also see from the below quote that the distinction between the two is often murky:

> "Odin threw Hel into Niflheim and gave her authority
> over nine worlds, on the condition that she shared
> all her provisions with those who were sent to her,
> namely men who die from disease and old age."[262]

For our purposes, it is worth considering swapping Helheim for Niflheim when journeying, or simply using the name Niflheim when describing Hel's realm. Certainly, it would help to get around the confusion with the cultural concepts of a Christian Hell.

What does Helheim look like? Within the *Voluspa* we have a description of:

> "A hall she saw standing far from the sun,
> On corpse-strand; it's doors look north;
> Drops of poison fall through the roof-vents,
> The halls is woven of serpents' spines"[263]

Within *Lokasenna*, Helheim is described as being "*down below the corpse-gates*"[264], Hel is far away from the warmth and life giving properties of the sun and faces the cold and dark north. A dog, Garm, guards the beginning of

---

[260] Nasstrom, *Freyja: The Great Goddess of the North.* 1995.
[261] Eiriksson, *Egil's Saga.* 2004.
[262] Faulkes, *Edda.* 1995.
[263] Larrington, *The Poetic Edda.* 1999.
[264] Ibid.

the road that leads to Hel. [265] Poison dropping from the roof makes it a place that is not habitable for the living. The corpse gates and serpent spines loom, giving us formidable imagery. This is all the more reason for us to think carefully before we decide to take the journey into Hel's realm as part of our seidr rites.

The imagery of the journey to Helheim is used by Hrafnar. Within the Norse literature, this journey is described in several places, predominantly within the Poetic[266] and the Younger[267] Eddas. As stated earlier, H.R. Ellis Davidson's The Road to Hel is an excellent resource for looking at the imagery of Helheim and journeying towards it. The imagery found within Norse literature is very similar to that found within descriptions of Orpheus' journey to the Underworld to find Eurydice[268] and within Odysseus' journey to the Underworld in order to meet with and speak to Patrocles.[269] The trading routes across Europe at this time, lead us to wonder whether it is likely that the author had access to these sources, or even just to the mythology found within them. More information on Hellenic borrowing can be found in chapter eight.

The journey to Helheim forms a large part of our high seat rite. The seer journeys to speak to the dead. The dead are found within Helheim. Not all of the entities that visit and speak during the high seat rite will be constant inhabitants of Helheim, but it is a good place to ask spirits to gather. Within our rite, the gates of Helheim are shown not as corpses, but as blocks of fire and ice that the seer must cross through to enter. This imagery came from a friend of mine, Swedish Academic Leila Wiberg, in 2001, shortly before her death in 2003. Drawn to leading a seidr rite at a pagan gathering, I had a few experiments and a very basic concept drawn together that was missing some very significant details. I asked Leila (who was also a very accomplished ritualist) for some suggestions on how to draw the seer into Helheim, and she came up with the fire and ice imagery that we find works so well during the rite.

As we saw in chapter one, the concept of a wall of fire (and of that wall of fire being cold) being a barrier between

---

265 Larrington, The Poetic Edda. 1999.
266 Ibid.
267 Faulkes, Edda. 1995.
268 Kerényi, The Heroes of the Greeks. 1978.
269 Homer, The Odyssey. 2003.

worlds does exist within the Norse literature.[270] The barrier separating the worlds is an important concept that shows that the worlds and their inhabitants do not easily collide. H.R. Ellis Davidson also gives examples of other myths that feature barriers that must be passed through in order to enter a supernatural realm. For example, Skirnir passes over a wall of flames on horseback. We are again reminded that within Greek mythology, the river Styx separates the land of the dead, with the supernatural ferryman the only person able to cross it to take the souls across.[271]

A hero journeying to the land of the dead is a common theme amongst European mythology. As well as Odysseus and Orpheus' travels in the Greek mythology, we can also find Achilleus making the journey, as well as Persephone who is queen of the realm of the dead for a part of the year. In Roman literature, Aeneas takes a similar journey to Odysseus,[272] and within Finnish mythology Vainamoinen visits the land of the dead in the *Kalevala*.[273] Although descent myths were common, J.G. Bishop writing in *The Journey to the Other World*, edited by H.R. Ellis Davidson, points out that: *"Descent journeys have much in common with ascents to heaven, as tales of Siberian shamans show"*[274] which reminds us that the underworld is not the only place that heroes visited. It is worth pointing out at this time that Helheim is not the only place that you can journey to in order to meet with and gain wisdom from spirits. Your rite needs to work for you and your group, so use elements that work for you.

THE DRUM

The drum is linked intrinsically to the seidr that I work with, although there is very little to suggest that it was used in the past by those working seidr. We find that most of the sources we know of put the emphasis onto the singing and the chanting;[275] and do not mention a drum of any kind. We should not be in any doubt that the Norse would have had access to some kind of drum, even just through their

---

270 Ellis, *The Road to Hel*. 1943.
271 Homer, *The Odyssey*. 2003.
272 Virgil, *The Aeneid*. 2003.
273 Lönnrot, *The Kalevala*. 1999.
274 Davidson, *Journey to the Other World: Papers from the Exeter Conference, 1971*. 1975.
275 Chisholm & Flowers (eds), *A Source-book of Seid*. 2002.

neighbours. The drum seems to be mentioned within *Lokasenna* as Caroline Larrington[276] translates the line discussing Odin's seidr work as *"and you beat on a drum as witches do"* which leads us to assume that the drum was used and that when it was it was associated with seidr. However, Stephen Flowers and James Chisholm translate the same line as *"and you struck on a chest like a seeress."*[277] (They give the root word of seeress as volva, a term that we investigate in the first chapter.) In brackets they use the word *'shrine'* after the chest. The difference between the three words *'drum'*, *'chest'*, and *'shrine'* is very wide. *'Drum'* gives Odin's act more of a shamanic focus, and links it with the Sami and Finnish ritual practice of their neighbours. *'Chest'* draws us the picture of a wooden box and its significance becomes a vessel that holds something inside or is simply used to make a noise. *'Shrine'* takes the focus onto the religious and links it with the practice of Utiseta and the idea of *'pounding the earth'* to wake the spirits.

The drum, for me, is a way of creating and altered state of consciousness, but also a way of ensuring that the group keeps the time of their journey together. The person holding the drum brings everyone together, keeps time, and uses the drum beat to then bring everyone back at the same time. The drum is not essential, and I believe that there are groups working seidr that don't use a drum at all, but it is an element that I find to be immensely helpful in my rites.

Instead of a drum, a seidr high seat rite (or any seidr rite) can instead use the voice to create the atmosphere and altered state that the drum would otherwise have created. The shamanistic traditions of the north have various ways of using their voices to create an altered state and to move and use energy and to change the atmosphere. Examples of this can be found within the yoiking of the Sami tribes[278] and within the throat singing of the Siberian tribes.[279] Moving further south, you can also see examples of how a rhythm can be created simply by using the voice by looking at the Scottish traditional mouth music and weaving songs.

---

276 Larrington, *The Poetic Edda*. 1999.
277 Chisholm & Flowers (eds), *A Source-book of Seid*. 2002.
278 Dubois, *Nordic Religions in the Viking Age*. 1999.
279 Hutton, *Shamans*. 2007.

According to Michael Harner in *Way of the Shaman*, the most efficient beat to journey to is four beats a second.[280] It is worth experimenting with this, as well as other beats to find the one that you find most beneficial to your rites. It is also worth looking at Gabrielle Roth's *Five Rhythms* technique and experimenting with some of her suggestions.[281] As discussed, not all seidr groups use the drum within their rituals, and not all use the drum ecstatically, but the general feeling seems to be that the drum works well, so why not use it?

THE VARDLOKKUR

"The women now formed a circle around the platform on which Thorbjorg was seated, Gudrid recited the chant so beautifully and well that no one who was present could say he heard a chant recited by a lovelier voice. The seeress thanked her for her chant, adding that many spirits had been drawn there now who thought it lovely to lend ear, the chant had been so admirably delivered – spirits who before had wished to keep their distance from us and give us no hearing. And now many other things are apparent to me which earlier were hidden from me as from many others."[282]

Vardlokkur is the name given to the songs and chants that form a part of the seidr high seat rite. As we can see from the quote from the *Greenland Saga* above, these can be essential to making the rite successful. Within the *Greenland Saga*, Thorbjorg asks for someone to sing her some Vardlokkurs. Halldis speaks up and says that, although she is Christian, she was taught some Vardlokkurs by her Finnish foster mother.[283] Vardlokkur loosely translates as spirit attractor or spirit caller and Jan Fries gives the meaning of *lokkur* as to lure or to entice.[284] Palsson translates Vardlokkur as Warlock Songs, strengthening their role in a number of seidr rites.[285] He translates Halldis' speech as *"I am neither a sorceress or a*

---

280 Harner, *The Way of the Shaman*. 1992.
281 Gabrielle Roth, *Ecstatic Dance*. 2004.
282 Jones, *Erik the Red and Other Icelandic Sagas*. 1961.
283 Fries, *Seidways*. 1996.
284 Ibid.
285 Palsson, *Voluspa*. 1996.

witch, but when I was in Iceland, my foster mother Halldis taught me spells that she called Warlock Songs.[286]

The role of the Vardlokkur in our high seat rite is predominantly to call the spirits, and to give them the energy they need to interact with the Seer and pass on their wisdom. The idea of a song *'waking'* the spirits can also be found in Harner, who says that *"Each shaman has at least one power song that he uses to "wake up" his guardian and other helpers to help him in healing and other work."* [287] Blain gives us another purpose for the Vardlokkur, which is that singing the songs *"gives the seeresses access to knowledge that is otherwise hidden."*[288] This is an idea that is backed up in the Latin text *Saxo Grammaticus* which talks about a seer who *"the power of her songs were so great that she seemed able to see into perplexing affairs however entangled with knots and far away, and be able to call out to the light."*[289] Lindquist writes a quote from an Yggdrasil practitioner, Marie who says that *"We realised from the start that the Vardlokkur, the songs to lure away the soul, were the most important."*[290] This is backed up by Harner who suggests that the power songs of a shaman can become a trigger which helps to shift the shaman into an altered state of consciousness.[291]

We can see from the quotes that the role of the Vardlokkur is far reaching. Firstly, it wakes and feeds the spirits, secondly it untangles knots and gives access to knowledge that is currently hidden, and thirdly it allows the soul to disengage from the body and begin to journey. If we look at the role of the Vardlokkur as feeding the spirits, we can see a similar practice within spiritualist churches, where the congregation sings hymns in order to raise the energy for the spirits to manifest for the medium. In *Arrow-Odd's Saga*[292] the Seer is accompanied by a large entourage of singers. Does the high number of singers suggest that part of the chanting was to raise energy rather than simply be atmospheric? The idea of using power songs as triggers to trance states is an interesting one. Certainly, the

---

286 Palsson, *Voluspa.* 1996.
287 Harner, *The Way of the Shaman.* 1992.
288 Blain, *Nine Worlds of Seid-Magic.* 2001.
289 Chisholm & Flowers (eds), *A Source-book of Seid.* 2002.
290 Lindquist, *Shamanic Performances on the Urban Scene.* 1997.
291 Harner, *The Way of the Shaman.* 1992.
292 Chisholm & Flowers (eds), *A Source-book of Seid.* 2002.

Vardlokkur that we use most often has become a trigger for high seat work. Songs and chants can very easily become triggers and sigils for magical workings. If you are interested in this area, it is worth reading Jan Fries' *Visual Magick*.[293]

What we aren't able to decipher from our primary sources is what the Vardlokkurs sounded like. If we had some examples of antiquarian Vardlokkurs it would be easier for us to reconstruct them. Were they melodious? The *Greenland Saga* suggests that the songs were lovely and beguiling, yet *Gongu-Hrolf's Saga* describes the incantations there as *'terrible sounds'*.[294] What tempo were they chanted in? Were they poetic? In the *Greenland Saga*, the person who knows the Vardlokkurs on the farmstead was taught them by her Finnish foster mother, therefore, should we look to traditional Finnish music for our answers? Traditional Sami music involves a specific kind of singing called Yoiking. The Christians converting the Sami people in the last few centuries taught them that the Yoiking songs were for calling up the devil and banned them. Does this hint at a spirit raising history, or is it simply the consequence of one religion trying to separate a culture from their former religious heritage? Another kind of chanting that can be found within the indigenous neighbours of the Norse was throat singing, which was found within the Siberian and Inuit tribes. Did the Vardlokkurs include elements of throat singing?

Again, it is impossible to know for sure, but what we can do is look at the role of the Vardlokkurs and also the traditional songs, poetry, and music of the Northern regions, and put together something that works for us. I believe that the Vardlokkurs of the past would have been energy raising and consciousness changing and that perhaps, similar to traditional Scottish music, would have had a consistent beat that took away the need for the drums we are looking so hard to find evidence for. Possibly they would have been wordless, but equally, they might have taken a similar style to the lyric poetry found within the *Eddas*.

The Vardlokkur that we use most often is:

The gate is open

---

[293] Fries, *Visual Magick: A Manual of Freestyle Shamanism.* 2000.
[294] Chisholm & Flowers (eds), *A Source-book of Seid.* 2002.

The time has come
The seer's work
Must be done

This was created back in the late 1990s by a friend of mine and I when we were just beginning to experiment with the high seat rite. I wonder if, back then, we could have ever realised that ten years on it would still be our Vardlokkur of choice. Interestingly, it is chanted in a way that creates a sound equivalent to the four beats a second that Harner gives as the best beat for creating an altered state of consciousness.[295]

When creating Vardlokkurs and music for seidr rites it is worth looking at the traditional folk music of the Norse regions and their neighbours and experimenting with what is consciousness-changing for the people you are working with. Remember that different parts of the rite might need a different style of music. The Scottish mouth music for example works very well during the energy raising part of the rite.

BRINGING THE SEER BACK

If you are journeying to the Underworld, or anywhere else for that matter, it is of course, important to work out how you are going to get back before you go! The same goes for when you are leading the rite and therefore taking your Seer on the pathworking into Helheim.

It is good practice within pathworkings and journeys to retrace the steps you take going into the pathworking back out again. This means that each time you change imagery or take a different path, you remember it and make sure that you go through the same steps when it is time to come back to consciousness. This is to ensure that each step of consciousness you moved out of, you move back into in the same way so that you are fully back to consciousness when you come out of your trance. Sometimes you hear, in shamanic circles, someone described as *'losing a bit of their soul'*; the best way to avoid this happening coming after a journey is to follow this advice. As the high seat rite can be quite a deep trance state, it is worth also making sure that you take other steps too. One of these is simply just calling the Seer by their name, whilst you are bringing them back

---

[295] Harner, *The Way of the Shaman.* 1992.

to their every day consciousness. Your name is something that is incredibly mundane and linked specifically to your body and your everyday life, which makes it incredibly grounding. It is also something that you are programmed to respond to, for example if you were doing something dangerous as a child, your parents would call your name. By using someone's name you are talking to their every day conscious, but also to their subconscious. Your name is something that immediately distracts and calls your attention and has done from the Perhaps this is why having someone's true name is having power over them, and perhaps this is why folklore tells us not to tell the fairies our names because then they might be able to distract us. Kenaz Filan and Raven Kaldera in *Drawing Down the Spirits*, explain how calling someone's name during a possession rite can instantly take them out of their trance and back to mundane consciousness.

> *"Being called by name can actually shake many horses out of possession and call them back to themselves."*[296]

Before you start leading a high seat rite, refer to the psychic first aid examples given in the introduction. These are for emergency situations mostly, but it is important to have a toolkit of these ready just in case.

Once the Seer is back, it is important to make sure that they are fully grounded, again, refer to the examples given in the introduction. Don't forget that you also need to make sure that everyone present in the rite knows how to ground and that they have grounded their excess energy and returned to their every day consciousness before they leave your presence.

GROUP SIZE

Over the last ten years I have been very lucky to have found a variety of wonderfully talented (and brave!) people to work with. Pretty much every step I have taken has been alongside others who have happily listened to me, encouraged me, and stepped into the unknown side by side with me. Over the last five years I have been lucky to work with a dedicated group of people who have put on regular

---

[296] Filan & Kaldera, *Drawing Down the Spirits: The Traditions and Techniques of Spirit Possession.* 2009.

high seat rituals and experimented with different seer techniques.

I have found that the high seat rite works best when the group is between six and ten people. The audience's role in the high seat rite is not only to ask questions, but also to help raise enough energy for the seer and the other to interact. Well practiced ritualists will manage this within a smaller group (the first ever high seat rite I attempted was with me and only one other person to act as the seer). A greater number of people generate a greater amount of energy. In this instance, surely then the more people the better? On one hand, this is correct, however, the more participants you have, the more difficult it is to establish rapport and keep everyone focused. It is also essential, where an audience is not experienced, to have enough people with experience to keep an eye on everyone. Where a group is fairly big, it also makes it difficult to find enough space for everyone to dance in.

When you are working with groups larger than ten people, there are a few adaptations you can make to ensure that things run effectively. The above ritual can be used with more people (the largest group we have used this particular rite with was just under forty) but there are a few things which start to cause concern.

The first is the difficulty of having large numbers of people trance drumming and dancing. This isn't so much keeping an eye on all of those people, although that could be a concern. The problem comes with the speed that the energy is raised and the fact that the more people are dancing and drumming the more enjoyable the dancing and drumming becomes, which is great, but not so good when you want to put the lid on the energy at some point and simmer it down to a level where you are able to conduct a seer rite. A participant in the group Yggdrasil states *"during ecstasy drumming, one wants to dance not journey"*.[297]

To avoid this situation, when a group gets larger than fifteen people, we put in a few adaptations to the rite given in this chapter. The first adaptation is that we create a core dancing group (the battery) of four or five people at the front of the ritual space, and these are the only people who are dancing ecstatically during the rite. They provide the energy

---

[297] Lindquist, *Shamanic Performances on the Urban Scene*. 1997.

for the Seer, acting as a battery pack for the Seer's journey, and as something for the audience members to concentrate on. The audience, instead of ecstatic dancing and drumming, sway and clap and chant the Vardlokkur. For some of the audience, this may mean that they do not enter the same depth of trance that they would have when using ecstatic trance, however for some audience members the opposite will be true and they may find that their trance is more intense. With a large amount of people, a slightly lessened trance state for the audience might also be helpful for you.

With a larger audience, some of the intimacy has gone from the rite which means that the intensity can be less. This is counteracted by using more of the theatrical aspects of the rite. The theatre helps to keep the audience focused, partly because it gives them something to look at and consider, but it also helps the audience to become and feel a part of the ritual. The atmosphere in the area you are working is incredibly important for this. By making it look dramatic, with smoky incense and candles, and with an impressive high seat, you are creating a scene that draws in the audience from the moment they enter your space. You could also consider having the seer already seated and covered by the hood, and the designated 'battery' dancers already dancing before the audience makes their way in. You could keep the seer's identity secret from the audience by not allowing them to meet before the rite starts (this also allows the seer time to prepare mentally for the task ahead). As part of this theatre, the Master of Ceremony could take a role in bringing the questioners to the seer and taking them back to their place in the audience afterwards.

When you are working with a large group there is likely to be a larger number of questions from the audience. With more than twenty participants, if every person asks a question, that is more than twenty questions for the seer to answer. As discussed earlier, a seer can only spend so long on their journey before they begin to tire. It is possible for an experienced seer to answer that many questions, but they will have needed to work up to that level gradually through practice (consider it to being underwater or long distance running, it is a skill that you need to keep working on to achieve). You also should not consider it as a definite that they will be able to answer that many questions if they have before. But what do you do about all of those questioners who are keen to have their questions answered?

One way to ensure more questions can be answered is to have more than one seer during the rite. The concern here is how to make the transfer seamlessly during the rite. By keeping both seers in Helheim, but allowing them to take turns, you keeping two people in Helheim for twice as long. The seers may be having a break from the seeing, but they are still in trance and still in the underworld. For the seer that is stepping down, they are no longer prophesising, but they are still in Helheim, and now they are both exhausted and in Helheim. Using the pathworking that we use to bring the seer out of Helheim and the new seer into Helheim could be distracting for the audience as it is fairly long and involves a lot of movement, but my suggestion would be that this would be the best way to do it, if you did decide to swap seers. A way to lessen the distraction for the audience would be to have the seers already sitting on their high seats and to give them the whole pathworking while seated, allowing the switch to be a quieter affair.

When we put on larger seidr high seat rites, we keep to one Seer and brief the audience not to expect that all of their questions will be answered.

THE RITE FOR WORKING IN PAIRS AND SMALL GROUPS

Although I have found that this rite seems to work best with six to ten participants, it is possible to work with smaller groups. For three to five participants you don't need to worry as much about putting watchers in place, as it is more likely that everyone in the group will look after each other (and they are more likely to know each other, and therefore know what is usual ritual behaviour for that person and what isn't). With less people it is sometimes the case that the energy raising takes longer, but the opposite can also be true, especially if the group mind is strong and each member is focused and ritually competent. It is worth looking at using a smaller space when you have a smaller group, but again, this is not essential. Another adaptation that you could make would be for the guide to be the only person that stays out of a deep trance and for the guide to lead all the members of the group into Helheim to communicate with the spirits gathered.

If you are working in a pair rather than a group, the rite automatically seems to take a less ecstatic and more conversational feel with the guide and Seer working very closely together. The guide leads the Seer to Helheim and then questions them whilst they are there. As there is only one person to ask the questions, often they then follow on from each other. It is likely, also, that you would need less of the theatrical props and paraphernalia. This might even stretch to the Seer not needing a High Seat.

WORKING SOLITARY

It is difficult to adapt this ritual to a solitary working, as the emphasis is on the questions and answers which, technically need someone to ask and listen to. However, the rites given in chapter one have a very similar flavour and you may be able to substitute the high seat rite for one of these. You could also take elements of this rite and blend them with the chapter one rites to make something that falls between the two.

THE HIGH SEAT: A RITE

> *It goes without saying now that these rites serve as examples which can be adapted and experimented with. This particular rite we have been practising in various forms since 2001, it certainly does not look the same now as it did then. It is almost guaranteed that in the future more changes are likely to have been made. The best rites grow and change with our needs. Borrow, experiment, adapt, but above all, enjoy.*

ROLES:

* *The Seer (who journeys to Helheim)*
* *The Master of Ceremonies (who leads the rite)*
* *The Watcher/s (keeping a watchful eye on the proceedings)*
* *The Battery (raising the energy)*
* *The Chorus (invoking the spirits)*
* *The audience (asking questions when directed to)*

* **Purification of the working space**, *an incense of frankincense, sage, and rosemary works well, you want the atmosphere nice and smoky.*
* **Invocation of the Disir circle** *(see chapter six)*
* **Invocation to Freyja**
* **Invocation to Odin**
* **Invocation to Hel** *and ask to enter her realm (be aware of the answer and act on it if needs be!)*
* **Raise energy for the rite** *(we do this via ecstatic dancing and drumming, with a bigger audience only the battery wildly dance and the audience sway and clap, but with a smaller group, everybody dances)*
* **The drumming quietens and everyone sits in a circle**
* **Invocation to the ancestors and spirits** *asking those who wish to give their wisdom to attend*
* **Visualisation of the world tree Yggdrasil** *in the centre of the space, its tall trunk stretching up, and its roots within Helheim. Within Yggdrasil is a spiral staircase: "As you sit a misty shape begins to form in front of you, in the centre of the circle, a tree trunk forms, wide and strong, reaching from the floor right up and through the*

ceiling. *This is an Ash tree, but not any Ash tree. Before you stands the tall tree Yggdrasil, the axis of the nine worlds. Yggdrasil holds a spiral staircase that journeyers from all worlds can use to travel. Now, Yggdrasil is being used to transport those who wish to impart wisdom to our Seer to travel to and congregate in Helheim in order to speak to the Seer when s/he travels there. They travel from wherever they usually reside, passing through Yggdrasil, but staying within its confines until they reach Helheim."*

* **All chant the Vardlokkur** *(we use "The Gate is open, the time has come, the seer's work, must be done' to a beat of four beats per second) During the Vardlokkur everyone sways and claps, while still seated.*

* **When the Seer is ready, they are given the staff and cloak and a pathworking to Helheim**. *The Master of Ceremonies keeps an eye on the Seer and decides when it is time to give them the pathworking. The drumming and the Vardlokkur chant quieten but never stop, not until the end of the rite. Only the Seer hears the pathworking: "You stand in a freshly ploughed field, amongst the soft, brown, soil. The land is flat and you can see for miles around you, but this is farming land so all you can see, right up to the horizon, is soft, brown, earth. A mist is forming just above the ground and it hovers like a dusting of snow. You feel the earth underneath your feet, soft and cool beneath your toes, and slowly, slowly you feel yourself beginning to sink. Deeper and deeper into the earth you sink. First your feet, then your knees, and then your waist. Sinking ever further into the soft brown soil. It feels cool and solid and you feel safe. The soil reaches your shoulders, and then your chin, your mouth, your nose, and your eyes. Until eventually, you are totally enveloped in the soft brown earth and it closes up above your head. Still further you sink, down, down; slowly sinking further and further into the soil until you realise that your feet have hit solid stone. This is the spiral staircase that takes you down to Helheim. Feel your feet tread each stone step, downwards, spiralling down and down."*

* **The Seer is led around physically walking in a spiral** *"As you reach the final few steps you know the gates of Helheim are close. Then you see the gates. Tall and imposing the gates are made of blocks of fire and ice.*

You must have courage to enter Helheim. Are you ready to enter?"

* **The Seer answers in the positive** *and the Master of Ceremonies physically pulls them forward, their journeying spirit enters the gates of Helheim. "Through FIRE, ICE, FIRE, ICE. You have passed through the gates. You are in Helheim. The High Seat is before you. Sit on it."*

* **The Seer is sat on the High Seat** *and asked what they can see. They describe anything that is obvious straight away to them.*

* **The Master of Ceremonies directs the questions:** *"Seer, are you ready for your first question?" While the Seer is on the High Seat, they are only referred to as 'Seer', never by their name. Each questioner starts their question by addressing the Seer "Seer," then their query. No question may be repeated (unless the Seer couldn't hear) and no clarification can be asked for. Questions should be clear and open, and of importance to the questioner.*

* **The Seer leaves Helheim,** *when the Master of Ceremonies feels that they are ready to go. The Seer is stood up, called by their name, and taken back through the pathworking – gates first, spiral staircase, and back up through the soil. At the spiral staircase, the cloak is removed and their mundane name is called.*

* **The Vardlokkurs and drumming stops**

* **The Seer is given food and drink and helped to ground**

* **The ancestors are thanked and asked to return through Yggdrasil**

* **Everyone grounds and food and drink is shared.** *Once all the energy has been grounded, it is a good idea for the Master of Ceremony to go around the circle and ask everyone to say their names. Look at their eyes, listen to the way they say their name, and judge whether or not you feel that they need any extra grounding. An experienced Master of Ceremony soon gains an almost sixth sense for this mini ritual.*

* **Time is allowed to share any response to particularly emotive answers**

* **Thank Hel and explain that the rite has ended**

* **Thank Odin and explain that the rite has ended**

* **Thank Freyja and explain that the rite has ended**

* **Take down the disir circle**
* **Ground and evaluate.** *Don't forget to encourage participants to write down what the Seer said to them, and any other thoughts and feelings they have. This should be done after the ritual, not during, to ensure that every participant continues to focus during the rite.*

CHAPTER FIVE

THE DEAD

As you will have no doubt realised, elements of contemporary and antiquarian seidr involved communication with spirits and ancestors. An easy way to classify these is under the chapter heading of *'the dead'*. When we look at the Norse relationship with the dead, it is important to remember that their concept of the soul and of death was slightly different to our concept.

THE SOUL

For the Norse, the soul was something that had different parts to it. In the same way that a part of you was able to leave your body and take another form, a part of you would stay with your body after death without meaning that you were not *'at rest'* and incomplete.[298]

> *"Still in Iceland today, death is not seen as something that is an abrupt break, rather it is the start of a process by which a person becomes increasingly removed from the everyday world."*[299]

We can see that death to the Norse did not mean that the soul instantly left the body and that person either ceased to exist, or journeyed to its afterlife in its entirety. The belief was held that a part of that person would continue to exist as energy at the place where they died. This then became their grave and depending on the

---

[298] Blain, *Wights and Ancestors*. 2000.
[299] Ibid.

importance of the person, a mound or cairn would be raised over them in order to honour and remember them.[300] A part of their soul and essence would live on in the lives of their kin and their down-line. Another part of their soul would live on in the *memories* of their kin.[301] This memory (and therefore this part of the dead person's soul) did not need to die with the person who remembered them, but could live on in the words and thoughts of others through being passed on as stories. This is where the *Sagas*, the stories of the Norse and their family history, come. The *Sagas* ensured that on a dark winter night, the memory of the ancestors was remembered and honoured. More than a thousand years later we still remember them and keep that part of their soul alive, every time we read, translate and repeat their *Sagas*. Another part of their soul journeyed to their afterlife resting place, be it Helheim, or Valhalla, or Freyja's hall Sessrumnir.

> "In family Sagas, to which we might turn to look for more naturalistic accounts of religious practice, there is a completely different picture of non-aristocratic afterlives. Insofar as an afterlife is envisioned at all, it seems to involve the dead living on in their burial mounds."[302]

If we consider the soul in this way then elements of this book, and especially of this chapter, begin to make more sense to us. Although culturally the West might not have this concept, similar beliefs can be found elsewhere. For example, there are Vodou traditions that believe that the soul has several parts and these parts are the ones that leave the body in order to make room for their spirits, the Lwa, when they are possessed.[303]

THE FYLGIA

The *fylgia* follows on from the concept of the hugr found in chapter three. The fylgia is often called the fetch or follower and is either considered to be a part of the soul, or it is considered to be a *"helping spirit"*[304] that is attached to

---

300 Blain, *Wights and Ancestors*. 2000.
301 Ibid.
302 O'Donoghue, *From Asgard to Valhalla*. 2008.
303 Filan & Kaldera, *Drawing Down the Spirits*. 2009.
304 Blain, *Wights and Ancestors*. 2000.

the soul, often at birth. The fylgia is often described as appearing in animal form and a person is able to send their fylgia out to *'work'* whilst their body and soul remains.[305] The Anglo-Saxons also had a version of the fylgia, which was the Watch or the Ward.[306] The fylgia's role seems to be an exploratory one, and it was believed that it would go on ahead of someone when travelling. There are stories that tell of households beginning to feel sleepy before a visitor arrives, and this is the fylgia, arriving at the house first. There are examples of people knowing that visitors are going to arrive unexpectedly because they begin to feel sleepy, and this sleepiness is caused by the arrival of the unexpected visitor's fylgia.[307] Stromback links this to the cat who knows when someone is about to arrive, proposing that they see the fylgia arrive before the person. Certainly, I have known many cats who are waiting for their owners before their arrival, despite their owner not coming home at a regular time or coming home way before their regular time.

Stromback suggests that the fylgia can be sent out from magicians when they are sleeping or in an ecstatic trance.[308] Is this why people were said to feel sleepy when an unexpected visitor was about to arrive? Was their fylgia leaving the body to acknowledge and investigate the arriving fylgia when it appeared? In *Havardr Saga*, two men are seen to be sleeping, whilst their fylgia battle with each other.[309] In *Sturlungasaga* a woman is warned to stay at home because there is a hostile fylgia around.[310] These examples back up the suggestion that the sleepiness is the fylgia freeing itself from the body in order to investigate and be prepared to upcoming battle if it needs to.

The concept of the fylgia is a very similar one to the hugr and links in with the shape shifting elements in chapter three. In the fylgia, we can see another part of the soul that might gain another job after death.

---

305 Blain, *Wights and Ancestors*. 2000.
306 Strömbäck et al., *Sejd*. 2000.
307 Ibid.
308 Ibid.
309 Ibid.
310 Ibid.

THE ANCESTORS

As a part of the dead was believed to live on in memories and stories, remembering and honouring the ancestors was an important part of Norse life. Within modern paganism, the idea of honouring and remembering your ancestors has not been taken up with as much vigour as some of the other pre-Christian beliefs. However, the heathen community has a much richer attitude to ancestor worship than many of the other modern pagan traditions who will often only remember the ancestors once a year at Halloween. It is fair to say that the ancestors were a much more relevant and remembered part of ritual life to the Norse (or could we say, to our ancestors?) than they are to us today. H.R. Ellis Davidson refers to instances where people would recite their ancestors and their places of burial.[311] How many of us are able to do this today? The names may not be passed on down the family line in the same way, but today we have access to so many more places to research and find out these facts. Whoever and whatever our ancestors were, which religious belief, which nationality, and which race; is it not also a good thing for us to learn names and places of burial to recite?

> *"Like the medium and the shaman, the volva was believed to converse with spirits, especially spirits of the dead, and to communicate to her living audience what they – he or she – told her."*[312]

We can see from the quote above that part of the Volva's role was communicating with the spirits and to ass what they said back to the living. Dronke refers to this role as being similar to the role of a medium or a shaman. Certainly, within the rites in this book, the ancestors and the dead play an important part. Ancestors were worshipped within the Nordic regions[313] and archaeological evidence in neighbouring Finland suggested that possibly offerings of food and other gifts were left for dead ancestors.[314] In Norway, when toasts were offered to the gods, there would also be toasts raised to their *"kinsmen who lay in the barrows"*.[315]

---

311 Davidson, *The Hill of the Dragon.* 1950.
312 Dronke, *Myth and Fiction in Early Norse Lands.* 1996.
313 Dubois, *Nordic Religions in the Viking Age.* 1999.
314 Ibid.
315 Ibid.

The Ancestors then, as we can see, were expected to be consulted for advice. As Fries says, *"Necromancy was an acceptable way of gaining information in the old North."*[316] If a person was wise in life, you can assume that they are likely to have just as many wise words in death. In neighbouring Siberia, shamans were considered to become even more powerful once they were dead.[317] Of course, if your ancestor didn't have great wisdom in life, it is likely that perhaps they won't be as helpful as someone who did, but realistically, who is going to care as much about your problems as your own ancestors? After all, you keep their bloodline and their memory alive. In my experience, the spirits and ancestors seem to live on a different timeline to us, and often information they give relates to something that becomes clear much later, maybe even years ahead in the future. If they have access to time in a different way to us, maybe they also have access to parts of our future that we can only guess at.

HONOURING THE ANCESTORS

The ancestors don't need to necessarily be honoured with grand rituals and gestures. The evidence from the Norse tells us that what they really want is to be remembered. The honour is the memory. Therefore, to truly honour our ancestors, learning about them and speaking about them is the best place to start. Try putting aside regular time to spend thinking and remembering those that you can, and finding out about the rest. As we can see from the Norse *Sagas*, those who are written about live on - so write down your memories and follow your relatives (who remember people you don't) around with voice recorders and notebooks. It is worth mentioning here that the Norse idea of kin did not only stretch to blood relatives; there are plenty of mentions in the *Sagas* (for example the *Greenland Saga*)[318] of foster families, and these family members are considered as fully as kin as the blood relatives.

---

316 Fries, *Seidways*. 1996.
317 Hutton, *Shamans*. 2007.
318 Jones, *Erik the Red and Other Icelandic Sagas*. 1961.

THE DEAD AND THEIR GRAVE MOUNDS

> *"That I advise you ninthly, that you bury corpses*
> *Where you find them on the ground,*
> *Whether they are dead of sickness or else drowned,*
> *Or men killed by weapons."*[319]

The Norse custom was to bury their dead wherever they died (or as the text above suggests where the body was found. If we consider the belief in a part of the soul lingering with the body, we can then question whether the soul was attached to the corpse itself, or to the place where it died. After burial, the grave was sometimes left unmarked, but very often it would have a mound raised over it. It too, could have had a stone cairn built on top.[320] The grave mounds themselves became important as memorials[321] and there are also instances where a person who had been lost at sea and therefore did not have a corpse, would have a grave mound raised for them as a memorial.[322]

The grave itself would often also contain objects that it was believed the dead could use in the afterlife.[323] Archaeological research has found things like swords, spindles, and jewellery accompanying the dead on their journey. There are also instances across Scandinavia (and as far south as the United Kingdom)[324] of boats being buried with people, full of grave goods.[325] Possibly time has eroded many of the other things that were buried for use in the afterlife, but *Laxdaela Saga* mentions some *"blue and evil looking"*[326] bones buried with a sorceress.

The Scandinavian landscape is still blessed with burial mounds, forming a clear reminder of the importance of them to our ancestors. The grave mound was an important factor in the honouring of the dead and of the ancestors, not only as a memorial, but as a place where you could be in contact with the person buried underneath. It could be suggested that there was a cult-like focus on the dead and

---

[319] Larrington, *The Poetic Edda.* 1999.
[320] Dubois, *Nordic Religions in the Viking Age.* 1999.
[321] Davidson, *The Hill of the Dragon.* 1950.
[322] Ibid.
[323] Dubois, *Nordic Religions in the Viking Age.* 1999.
[324] See the Sutton Hoo exhibition in the British Museum.
[325] Davidson, *The Hill of the Dragon.* 1950.
[326] Palsson, *Voluspa.* 1996.

the grave mound.[327] Chapter one describes Odin being able to call up and talk to a dead Volva by using her corpse and grave mound. There are also instances of the Norse Kings giving important rulings and claiming their inheritance from the grave mound of the past King.[328] Through the belief in being able to gain wisdom from the dead, the grave mound also became a place of *'mantic inspiration'* that, as time went on, became associated more with the mound itself than with the wisdom of the person that was buried within it.[329] The grave mound, then, became associated with the Seer. Within England, meetings and assemblies were often held on mounds.[330] We can see elements of this belief as far West as the Celtic Kingdom of Wales, where the *Book of Llandaff* describes a Welsh King signing over land whilst being physically on the tomb of the former King. The original meaning of the word *'Gorsedd'* which is a Welsh word associated with poetry and celebration, was *'high seat'*.[331]

Unsurprisingly, the respect and interest in the dead and their graves was something which didn't sit so well with the new Christian religion, and as Christianity began to spread, the tales of the grave mound began to take a more sinister turn.[332] Corpses began to return from the dead without the help of seidr workers. In *Egil's Saga* a dead man rose at night so often that they needed to burn his body.[333] In *Grettirs Saga*, the hero fights the occupant of the grave mound for the treasure buried inside it.[334] King Hrapp, after a successful series of hauntings, was unearthed to find that his corpse had not decayed.[335] In *Laxdaela Saga* Herdis dreams that a Seer comes to give her a message, this message is from a woman who is upset that her grandmother keeps disturbing her. It turns out that this is a seeress who is buried in a place in the church that Herdis' grandmother kneels on to pray. The bones are then

---

327 Ellis, *The Road to Hel.* 1943.
328 Davidson, *The Hill of the Dragon.* 1950.
329 Ellis, *The Road to Hel.* 1943.
330 Davidson, *The Hill of the Dragon.* 1950.
331 Blain, *Wights and Ancestors.* 2000.
332 Dubois, *Nordic Religions in the Viking Age.* 1999.
333 Eiriksson, *Egil's Saga.* 2004.
334 O'Donoghue, *From Asgard to Valhalla.* 2008.
335 Dubois, *Nordic Religions in the Viking Age.* 1999.

moved to a place where they are less likely to be disturbed.[336]

The dead returning as walking corpses is also found in other *Sagas*[337] and was such a well known phenomena that it was given the terms *Draugr* and *Hamr*, both being used to describe ghosts and animated corpses.[338] The concept of walking corpses and restless dead (especially those that were not buried properly or were disturbed after dead) may have travelled with the trade routes from the Greek. These are common themes within Greek literature.[339] A parallel that can be drawn from a modern perspective is with vampires, which have captured the popular imagination for the last few centuries. Another parallel is with the Christian Saints, whose bodies also were said not to decay and who also were able to influence and give wisdom from the grave.

UTISETA

Directly linked to the concept of the soul and the grave mound is the Norse practice of *Utiseta* or sitting out to give its most common translation.[340] This was where someone looking to gain wisdom, often to prophesise or to make a decision, would spend the night out of doors. Utiseta often took place specifically on grave mounds, and as we learnt earlier in this chapter, the mound itself was often seen as more significant than the person buried underneath, especially in later years. Utiseta was a practice that continued right up to and post-Christianity.[341] Ursula Dronke refers to this practice as *'spirit listening'* and tells us that it was a common Germanic practice.[342]

As we can see from the below quote by Adalsteinsson in *Under the Cloak*, Utiseta was often very strongly linked to sorcery and to *'waking the dead'* in order for them to give you information.

> *"According to the sources, 'sitting out' appears to have taken two forms in particular. On the one*

---

336 Magnusson et al., *Laxdaela Saga*. 1975.

337 Gylfason, *Njal's Saga*. And *Orkneyinga Saga*. 1998.

338 Strömbäck et al., *Sejd*. 2000.

339 Ogden, *Greek and Roman Necromancy*. 2004.

340 Fries, *Seidways*. 1996.

341 Blain, *Wights and Ancestors*. 2000.

342 Dronke, *Myth and Fiction in Early Norse Lands*. 1996.

hand, the necromancer may be active, he chants spells and uses other means to summon the dead from their places in order to obtain from them whatever information was desired. On the other hand, he is inactive, he listens to the sounds of nature and is on the lookout for the visitation of spirits of the night."[343]

Utiseta then, was also about communing with the spirits of nature. Whilst communing with nature, a grave mound may not be necessary, and certainly the body inside the grave would not be required. It is also worth remembering that Norse grave mounds, although graves and therefore closely related to graveyards, were (and still are) thought of differently to the British concept of graveyards. Within Scandinavia, grave mounds are part of the landscape and are places to visit and take picnics (much the same as some of our British burial chambers). Therefore, to spend the night on a grave mound communing with nature is thought of in a very different way to spending the night in a graveyard.

The idea of gaining wisdom from listening to the spirits whilst spending the night outside is one that has made it into contemporary heathen and pagan belief. Utiseta, or spending the night outside communing with nature, can be found in the Vigil which is often undertaken as a rite of passage within modern paganism, and especially within Druidry.[344]

The vigil, or utiseta is not just found in the Norse - Scottish, Welsh, and Irish literature from a similar time also have examples of Seers going out into nature to prophesise. The Welsh Awenyddion (written about by Gerald of Wales)[345] went into the woods. The Irish and Scottish Seers have been discussed in chapter two. Adalsteinsson has also found a Norse version of the Irish Seers wrapping themselves in bull hides:

> *"There is an instance of a man lying a whole night wrapped in a hide in a secluded place to gain information. In folk tales collected by Jon Arnasson*

---

[343] Adalsteinsson, *Under the Cloak*. 1979.
[344] Carr-Gomm, *The Druid Way*. 1993.
[345] Cambrensis, *The Journey Through Wales and the Description of Wales*. 2004.

in the 19th century this is considered an accepted method when 'sitting out'."[346]

Whether Utiseta was being used to simply commune with and gain wisdom from nature spirits, or whether it was being used to actively awaken a corpse and summon the dead, we can see that it was an important rite within pre-Christian Scandinavia. As such, it has taken its place within contemporary heathen practice.

THE VIGIL

Despite the difficulty in many urbanised areas of finding somewhere suitable, the Vigil remains an important rite of passage for many contemporary pagan traditions. If we link the Vigil to Utiseta it becomes a very long standing tradition.

What do you learn from sitting out? Firstly, the absence of modern day distractions really helps to allow you to think clearly and organise your thoughts. Decision-making is a great time to use Utiseta as it gives you plenty of time in the Wilderness to reflect. Absence of electricity, and manmade light and noise pollution really does help to commune with the other – deity, spirits, ancestors, nature. Perhaps just as importantly, sitting out for the night doesn't allow you the distractions of needing to do something else, or of only focusing for a couple of hours before deciding to do something else. Spirit-listening takes time and concentration, and sitting out for a night or longer gives you that concentration. Of course, sitting out does not have to be just for the evening: a full weekend or several days is even better.

Sadly, depending on where you live, the practical aspects of the Vigil often mean that it is incredibly difficult to plan and organise. If you are lucky enough to live somewhere with lots of countryside and not many people, and have vast areas of forest and/ or open spaces (or even a few grave mounds scattered about) that are very rarely visited, then you are very lucky! Within Urban Britain few of these areas exist and those that do are visited fairly regularly. Dog walkers, doggers, campers, and day trippers litter our countryside, and if they weren't difficult enough to avoid, we also have an increasing amount of ritual

---

[346] Adalsteinsson, *Under the Cloak.* 1979.

attending and vigil questing pagans vying for the same *'quiet'* and *'untouched'* spots as us. You might find your perfect spot, plan it meticulously, and end up being beaten to your vigil.

The best way to make sure that you are undisturbed is to do your research really well. The less information available about your sacred Utiseta spot, the more likely you are to be alone. If your internet research brings up pages and pages of folklore and ghost stories, you need to either be aware that you might be interrupted, or you need to look for somewhere else. Similarly, make sure you check whether the space is one well known as an area people like to use for outdoor sex or you are likely to get more than you bargained for! Visit your place several times at the time you plan to make your Vigil; if it is always quiet and empty then you have more likelihood of an undisturbed Vigil. Check out, if you can, who owns the site and whether it has public right of way. If you do live somewhere that you know it will be more difficult to find peace and quiet within, put together a plan for what happens if you are disturbed. At least then you won't be put off if it does happen.

Of course, following on from this is the safety aspect. Clearly, you don't want to be surrounded by mobile phones, battery torches and cars, but you need to make sure that you have things to hand if you need them. Think through the safety angles and pre-plan what steps you will take if you do find yourself in danger. Always tell someone where you are going to be, and if possible have them nearby and ready to come and get you if you need them to. Having said all of this, don't let fear and suspicion stop you from getting the best out of your vigil.

Don't forget your spiritual safety. Call up your personal protection in the same way as you would for any other ritual and take any precautions that you would usually take. Decide what you want to achieve from your Vigil. For example, an answer to a question, further knowledge about the area you are working in, communion with specific spirits, or simply not being afraid. Be aware though, that often the removal of fear comes from facing your fear and you are likely to find yourself face to face with it either spiritually or physically, so remember the motto *'be careful what you wish for'* and don't ask for anything that you can't handle.

Waking the Spirits Rite

> *This is a slightly more active version of the Vigil, going into nature and calling up/ waking the spirits so that you are able to commune with them. The first thing to remember when putting together your own version of this rite is to make sure you know why you are doing it and what you are hoping to achieve. What questions are you looking for the answers to, what kind of spirits are you hoping to wake to ask, and why are they in a better position to tell you than others?*
>
> *Reasons that you might want to use a ritual like this would be if you intend to put some energy into earth healing and want to know how to do it, or if you are investigating the cause of supernatural disturbances. Another reason could be that you want to learn about a particular place or area, especially if you have unanswered questions. It goes without saying that if, when choosing your area to sit out and wake the spirits, you choose a grave mound or graveyard then you should expect to explain to its inhabitants why you are seeking to wake them, and for that to be a good enough reason!*
>
> *This rite involves the pounding of the earth found within the first chapter, and used by Odin to wake the Volva. Fries suggests that pounding the earth wakes the dead who reside beneath it, as well as insinuating that they should 'come HERE'.*[347]

* **Purify yourself**, *using your favoured method. My personal preference would be to use appropriate runes.*[348] *The purification is focused on yourself rather than the working space, because the intent of the rite is to enter someone else's space and therefore purifying the area is not appropriate.*
* **Use a gateway**, *either through creation of one using twigs/ markings on the ground (make sure you are environmentally friendly here), or by using a gateway that already exists (stile, gate, or natural gateway such*

---

[347] Fries, *Seidways*. 1996.
[348] Gerrard, *Odin's Gateways*. 2009.

as overlapping trees for example) to designate the start of your rite. Once you pass through the gateway you enter ritual time and space.

* **Invoke personal protection**, *again the disir circle is a good one to use.*

* **Call to the spirits that you want to invoke**, *making sure that your intent is clearly defined and that you are being specific about WHAT you want to invoke and WHY.*

* **Tell them of the offering that you are giving them to help you**, *and as with all exchanges, don't let them decide what to take.*

* **Raise energy to help the spirits to manifest**, *see chapter nine for a full breakdown of this but food, drink, singing, drumming, dancing, are all appropriate methods to use.*

* **Use your staff to pound the earth to wake the spirits**, *you can also use Vardlokkurs.*

* **Drum** *yourself into an altered state of consciousness, allowing the energy of the area and the spirits to take you to the answers - whether that is by the conversations forming within your mind's eye, through a journey, or through natural occurrences (wind, presence of birds/animals) which form oracles.*

* **Give the spirits your offering, if it wasn't already part of the energy raising**.

* **Thank the spirits for their wisdom**. *At this stage you could let them know that the rite is over and leave, or you could let them know that you will be staying overnight and thank them again in the morning when you are about to leave.*

* **Pass back through the gateway** *at the end of the rite, whether that is the next morning or immediately afterwards.*

* **On returning home**, *make sure that you are fully grounded and check for any stowaways who might have tried to come back with you. Use your gate or front door as the barrier to your own space and make sure that you leave anything that doesn't belong with you outside.*

* **Ground and evaluate**, *writing down any information you gained. Electric lights, television, and breakfast are all wonderful ways to help you gently back to the mundane.*

CHAPTER SIX

THE OTHER

The Norse concept of spirits, and *'other'* as we can see, wasn't simply limited to the dead. Of course, the Norse also had concept of deity, gods and goddesses who were worshipped and who would take an interest in your life. There were a myriad of other beings, however, who were neither dead nor deity but were something in between.

> *"All Nordic peoples recognized a range of spirits dwelling in particular objects or places, such as stones, trees, groves, waterfalls, houses, and small idols. Such deities were common throughout northern Europe."*[349]

These beings could be a part of nature, be attached to people and families, or to places, or they could be found on the battlefield (for example as Valkyrie).

THE DISIR

The *disir* were female spirits who were attached to a person (or more commonly to a family) and were responsible for protecting and guarding. Your disir were important to your wellbeing and safety. At birth a person might be attributed a collection of disir and these would stay with them throughout their life. They would also have disir that were responsible for the wellbeing of the whole of their family. It is unclear whether these disir were ancestors who had undertaken the role of disir after death, or whether these were similar to Norns, who were responsible for

---

[349] Dubois, *Nordic Religions in the Viking Age.* 1999.

fate.[350] The disir were often linked with the Norns, with people being said to receive their own personal and family Norns at birth.

> *"The Scandinavian spirits of the household and fate, the disir and nornor – derive ultimately from ancestor worship: a bride brought her clan's ancestral spirits with her when moving to her husband's home."*[351]

As we can see from the above quote from Dubois, the disir, as well as being female, were also very much associated with women. He also links them intrinsically with ancestor worship, which allows us to suggest that possibly their origin (and the origin of individual disir) might have been ancestral. One of the most important roles of the disir was to keep women and their babies' safe in childbirth.[352] Prayers and offerings were made to the disir for the safe release of children from women.[353] The Norns were also invoked during childbirth, as well as the goddess Frigga.

The disir had their own blots (sacrifice/feast days) within the Norse calendar. This disirblot was taken very seriously and it was believed to have taken place between Autumn and Winter.[354] Britt-Mari Nasstrom believes that it would have taken place between at the beginning of October for Winter Nights.[355] This rather helpfully links it to happening at a similar time to the much publicised and popularised Celtic feast of the dead, Samhain, otherwise known as Halloween. During this time of year, the British also have a celebration, Remembrance Day (11:00 on the 11th November, in memory of the end of the First World War). Dubois refers to disirblots happening at midwinter[356] (Swedish midwinter is 13th December rather than 21st December as it is in the British Isles). The importance of the disirblot is highlighted in *Njal's Saga*, where Thidrandi *"dies as a result of improper behaviour on the night of the ritual, falling victim to the disir when he breaks a taboo against opening the door."*[357]

---

350 Nasstrom, *Freyja*. 1995.
351 Dubois, *Nordic Religions in the Viking Age*. 1999.
352 Larrington, *The Poetic Edda*. 1999.
353 Ibid.
354 Nasstrom, *Freyja*. 1995.
355 Ibid.
356 Dubois, *Nordic Religions in the Viking Age*. 1999.
357 Ibid.

Working with the disir

We can see how important honouring the disir was to the Norse. You will also have seen the role that the disir play in many of my rites. The disir's role is to watch out for you and your fate, therefore getting to know your disir and working with them is a very good idea, especially if you want to invoke them for protection. Like the ancestors, I have found that the disir like to be remembered and spoken about. Blain suggests that a good way to do this is to make a list of our ancestors and forefathers and mothers that we do know and voicing this as part of a disir offering.[358] Remembering names and telling stories, as we saw in chapter five, is a good way of continuing to add honour and memory. Regularly giving offerings is another way to keep the disir around you. Those offerings can take the form of food, drink, incense, stories, time, or even promises. Regular can be anything from every time the moon is in a certain cycle, to an annual promise to remember and honour your disir at a disirblot. The ideal time for this to take place is when Autumn is moving into Winter, and using the timing of a popularised festival (such as Halloween or Remembrance Day, or even Christmas Eve which may have originally been the time of Mother's Night, which links in closely with the disir.) will help you to remember it.

---

[358] Blain, *Wights and Ancestors.* 2000.

MEETING THE DISIR RITE

> *This is a simple rite with journey to look at meet with and learn more about your disir. My preference when working with my disir, is to work indoors at home, as the disir are part of your life and are strongest where your energy is strongest, which is usually in your home or if you share a space, in your bedroom.*

* **Purify your space**, *using your preferred method.*
* **Invoke your disir,** *asking for them to come forward and make themselves known to you during this rite.*
* **State intent of ritual**, *which is likely to be getting to know and honouring your disir.*
* **Create an altered state of consciousness**, *my personal preference would be to start this rite with a Vardlokkur written for the disir, accompanied by swaying and drumming, and incense.*
* **Use the drum to journey**, *taking yourself into the heart of your homestead and using a gateway (for example visualising a door or some stairs that are not there in the mundane) to take yourself to a long corridor with many doors. See each doorway as containing a time in history, and journey into them one by one, speaking to the disir found behind it and learning their stories. Remember to use the corridor as the step between the times, and when returning remember to use your gateway back into your home.*
* **Honour each disir whose names you learnt or whose faces you were shown enough to name yourself with a toast**, *use the alcohol that is appropriate for your family and culture. Mead is traditionally Norse, but ale, cider, and wine are good too.*
* **Make an offering to your disir**, *suitable offerings are discussed above, but your disir are personal to you so will you know better than anyone which offerings are likely to be appropriate. If you are making promises, it is essential that you keep them.*
* **Give thanks to your disir and explain that the rite is over.**

* **Ground any excess energy and write down your experiences so that you can use the information the next time you honour your disir.**

DISIR BLOT

To honour your disir with a blot, you can use a similar role to the one given above. You may want to spend more time raising energy for them to use, and less time journeying to and communing with them. It is always worth spending some time journeying and speaking to your disir, just to make sure that there isn't anything that they need you to know or do at this point. Disir, like many Norse energies, are not known for their subtlety and if they need to get a message across or remove you from possible danger, you can assume that they won't be subtle about that either. If you have ever found yourself in the wrong place, only to have realised that actually this is the RIGHT place (especially as the place you were supposed to have been is seeing problems that you really didn't want to be caught up within) then you know that your disir have been unsubtly looking out for you. I thank and acknowledge my disir for a very complicated situation which meant that I was well away from the tube train I should have been on when the London bombs went off in 2005 ... however confused I was at the time!

THE DISIR CIRCLE

The Disir circle appears in the High Seat Rite in chapter three. It is a technique that I use when working with spirits and entities and has always served me well so far. When working with 'the other' it is important not to protect the space in such a way that keeps that which you are planning to work with outside of it. It also isn't practical to list the names of what you want to work with, as ancestors and spirits tend to be a lot more fluid than this, and often the most helpful contact of the rite could have been something that you hadn't expected to attend. Besides, if you can list all of your ancestors and their associates by name and remember each one in ritual then you are almost certainly in the minority! On the other hand, you don't really want to just hold the doors wide open and ask anything and anyone that is passing if they want to come along for a chat. It isn't good magical or spiritual practice, partly because you might end up with something that could be potentially damaging to you, but mostly because some things can waste time and take energy from your rite.

The disir circle simply is a barrier of your disir and the disir of the others attending the rite that holds and keeps out anything that you have asked it to on that occasion. Think of them as psychic bouncers if you will.

The clause *'or anything that we are unable to deal with at this time'* is used as a safety net because when dealing with entities we might find that we are dealing with an entity or a concept that is the source of much grief and confusion for someone. This may not be something that technically causes *'harm'*, but it is possible that the timing is not right for that person to face it at the moment, and also that the appearance might disrupt the ritual.

The idea of using something other to guard and protect your rite is not new in any way, shape or form. Perhaps it has been slightly forgotten in contemporary paganism, but there are groups who use entities rather than their own energy to protect their rites. As a comparison, many Vodou rites start with the invocations of saints and lwa *"whose role is to protect the space"*[359] as well as taking more active parts in proceedings. You could also ask the deities you are invoking to help protect and keep the rite focused, although it is likely that this would not be their only part in the rite. Your disir and any other guardian spirits that you have are supposed to look after you and look out for your safety. Why invoke something else to do this job when they are there already and have much practice in this area.

To cast the disir circle, I use a wooden knife, crafted by a friend of mine from a piece of bog wood.[360] This item was originally made for a re-enactment group but was never paid for and therefore never collected. I fell for its charms on sight and as soon as I picked it up, I felt as though it was made for me. If you use ritual tools, you will be able to find something that works for you, if you don't, you will be able to find other methods that already work for you under different circumstances.

Using the wooden knife, I create a boundary that designates my ritual area, by walking around the area with the knife. I walk around three times, while saying the following:

---

[359] Filan & Kaldera, *Drawing Down the Spirits*. 2009.
[360] Stagman Creations, West Wales.

"Sisters, Mothers, Grandmothers, Daughters,
Bear Mothers, Warrior Women, Ancestors
Those who have gone before us
Those who have always been
I call to you as our kin
Three times I call out for you to come to us
Three times, encircle our rite
Watch over us and focus our work
Let nothing come into this space that will cause harm
to us
Or that we cannot deal with at this time.
Sisters, Mothers, Grandmothers, Daughters,
Three times we have called you,
Three times stand strong and firm for us
And three times, we bid you welcome."

If you are using the disir for protection, it is also worth factoring in a time during the rite to make an offering to them.

THE NORNS

"From there come three girls, knowing a great deal
From the lake which stands under the tree;
Fated one is called, Becoming another
.... Must-be the third;
They set down laws, they chose lives,
For the sons of men the fates of men." [361]

The Norns within Norse mythology are three women who are responsible for the fates of humanity. They weave the web of wyrd, into which all fates are woven. Everyone has their own personal fate, called *orlog* [362] which is born with them and carried with them throughout their lives. It is woven with that of others, creating a web of fates, but a person's Orlog remains their own. [363] A person's Orlog threads are woven into Wyrd, interacting with, touching, and skipping those of others. Every action, every deed, every word, twisted into the great web. Wyrd's web has many strands, interwoven with complicated and simple pathways and patterns. Some fate strands lie strong and

---

361 Larrington, *The Poetic Edda.* 1999.
362 Blain, *Wights and Ancestors.* 2000.
363 Chisholm & Flowers (eds), *A Source-book of Seid.* 2002.

straight, some twist and turn, and some a circular repeating and returning.

The wool that the Norns weave into their web is spun by the goddess Frigga, who we shall see in more detail in chapter seven. The contemporary ideal of past, present and future is often assimilated into the contemporary heathen concept of the Norns, and as a concept the two are very similar. The translations of the individual Norn's names, however, are slightly differing from past, present, future. The Norse is Urd, Verdandi, and Skuld. Three iconic names that in the quote above, translated by Caroline Larrington, and are translated as Fated, Becoming, and Must Be. These titles give a real feeling of something that is unchangeable. *'Fated'* is not simply *'the past'* or *'what happened'*, it clearly gives no place for choice or chance, but states that the past is fated, planned and acted out. *'Becoming'* is the second Norn. The present is happening now, but more than that, it is actualising – becoming. The name suggests that which was planned and decided is gathering shape and form. *'Must Be'* is the title of the youngest Norn, written by the past and given shape and form by the present, Must Be is inevitable. It is waiting.

Elsa Brita Titchinell in her book *The Masks of Odin* gives a slightly different translation:

> *"One was named Origin, the second Becoming; these two fashioned the third, named Debt."*[364]

The differences between the meanings of Origin and Fated are clear. Titchinell has taken the inevitability out of the first Norn, and replaced it with an idea of beginnings. The use of the word Origin adds weight to the importance that the Norse placed on kinship and the land, origin is not simply what you did, but what gave you the energy and the being to do it. The third Norn is translated by Titchinell as *Debt*. The word is less inevitable than Larrington's *Must Be* but it holds far more onto the attitude that the past writes the future.

Larrington's translation of Fated gives the entire web of wyrd a strong element of being unable to be changed. The yarn has been woven, the threads have been cut, now we must complete it. Titchinell's translation allows more room for choice. The actions of Origin lead into Becoming, and together create the Debt. Debt allows us to see that the

---

[364] Titchenell, *The Masks of Odin.* 1968.

choices made in the past write the future, yet the great potential and glamour of the future is still marked heavily with an overlay of inevitability. Debt is not choice, debt is written, and debt is waiting to claim her time.

If we consider the Norse concept of the Norns in relation to contemporary paganism, and to witchcraft in particular, we can see that the idea of twisting and changing your future may not sit within the Norse boundaries. However, within the Norse literature, we can see that seidr and witchcraft is used, but instead of attempting to change what Must Be, it instead slows it down, or speeds it up. Baldr's death and the slow reckoning of Ragnarok[365] are two myth cycles that clearly display these traits. Therefore, in our own work with the Norns we need to recognise their link with what has to be. If you want to ask for your life to be changed or you want to change the inevitable, the Norns are not the right people to ask. If you want to face and understand your fate and catch a glimpse of what your *Must Be* is *Becoming*, a Norns rite is a good place to start.

Before we look at a Rite invoking the Norns, we should consider what or who writes fate. Who is responsible for deciding the Orlog of a person? Is it themselves and their actions? Or is it their family (their kin)? Do the Norns decide it as they weave the web? Is this web woven before birth or on an ongoing basis? Are the decisions of fate taken by Frigga whilst she spins the wool?

---

[365] Crossley-Holland, *The Penguin Book of Norse Myths.* 1996.

Asking the Norns, a Rite

> This is a variation on the Calling up the Volva Rite but involves three Volvas, each of which has a Norn invoked into them. Working with the Norns as part of a seidr high seat rite is a common theme within contemporary heathen groups, with Blain featuring the concept in Nine Worlds of Seid-Magic.[366] From my experience with this rite, the Norns make up a trio with a strong group mind formed between the three Norn Volvas. Before we trialled this rite we were wondering whether to direct the question to individual Norns or to them all, and what would happen if they all answered at the same time. In reality, the three Volvas embodying the Norns feel linked. Although they are three energies with three bodies, the distinction is blurred with the Norns finishing each others sentences and laughing in unison. The idea that one might talk over another is not something to worry about.

* **Purify the space** *using an appropriate incense.*
* **Invoke personal protection** *(e.g. the disir circle from chapter six)*
* **Invocation to the Norns** *(see chapter seven)*
* **State the intent of your rite**, *for example "We invoke the Norns in order to gain wisdom and understanding of our Orlog and the web of Wyrd, I give this offering." Again, don't expect to get anything from the Norse entities without offering something in return. If you don't offer, don't be surprised to find that they take. Offerings can be in the form of food, drink, incense, time, or a task.*
* **Chant the names of the Norns to raise energy**, *this can be accompanied by drumming/ dancing/ swaying, and works well as a spinning around with a designated group of chanters performing each Norn in an appropriate tone.*
* **Invoke the Norns into the Seers**, *visualising the energy of each Norn swirling and circling into the Seer. The Norns seem to enter gradually, as though being spun or woven piece by piece.*

---

[366] Blain, *Nine Worlds of Seid-Magic.* 2001.

* **Give offering of wine to the Volvas/ Norns,** *red for Urd, rose for Verdandi, and white for Skuld.*
* **The audience ask the Norns questions**
* **Once you have got your answers,** *give any promised offerings to the Norns, and explain that the rite has ended.*
* **Ground the Norns out of the Volvas,** *this might take a little time, with the Norns removing themselves in the same spinning, weaving way that they entered the Volvas.*
* **Thank the Norns again and reiterate that the rite is over.**
* **Ground and evaluate,** *making note of any answers given that you want to remember.*

CHAPTER SEVEN

THE GODS

THE NORSE DEITIES

There are many books available on the Norse pantheon, as well as books available on individual deities. Descriptions of myth cycles and attributes can all be found in both academic and practitioner texts, therefore I have kept my descriptions of the Gods brief with the view that those who have not already researched the deities of the North will be able to do so quickly and with ease. My recommendation for exploring this area would be to get *Edda* by Snorri Sturluson[367] as a primary text, and *The Penguin Book of Norse Myths* by Kevin Crossley Holland[368] as a secondary retelling.

The Norse deities came from two tribes, the Aesir and the Vanir. The Aesir were ruled by the God Odin, who was married to Frigga. The mythology talks of a war between the Aesir and the Vanir, with hostages being exchanged. Thus Njord, Freyja and Freyr from the Vanir came to live with the Aesir in their realm, Asgard. The Norse gods formed a pantheon in a similar way to the Graeco Roman deities, and whilst it is clear that some of the literature (for example the *Eddas*)[369] is written for entertainment rather than to document the gods, it is also clear from some of the *Sagas*

---

[367] Faulkes, *Edda*. 1995.
[368] Crossley-Holland, *The Penguin Book of Norse Myths*. 1996.
[369] Faulkes, *Edda*. 1995.

that the Norse people believed in and actively worshipped their gods.[370]

This chapter seeks to look at the Norse gods in the context of seidr and witchcraft and therefore focuses heavily on possession rites. Perhaps the most well known group to practice possession rites using the Norse deities is Diana Paxson's Hrafnar.[371] Using her knowledge and experience of the Umbanda community in San Francisco, Paxson borrowed elements of the voodoo format of trance and deity possession to honour and work with her own deities. Umbanda is a syncretic religion that mixes African and Catholic belief in a similar way to Voodoo.[372]

However, looking at the primary sources of Norse literature, we can see that perhaps this concept is not a brand-new one and that our Norse forebears did in fact have their own, now long forgotten, tradition of deity possession. Perhaps the most well-known of these examples comes from *Saxo Grammaticus*[373] description of Freyr rites: in *Volsungasaga*, Odin is described as visiting a chieftain whilst wearing the *'look'* of another chieftain.[374] The most helpful in describing what is possibly possession, however, is *Gautrek's Saga*.[375] In *Gautrek's Saga* a man takes part in a ritual where his father becomes Odin and another friend becomes Thor. Of course, we cannot be certain that these examples are describing possession, especially as we are looking at them with a bias that comes from knowledge of contemporary possession rituals, but certainly, it is not too narrow a step to suggest that it could be deity possession that we are witnessing here. In *Volsungasaga* we see Odin borrowing the look (the body?) of a chieftain in order to go and communicate with another chieftain. Also in *Volsungasaga* we see a sorceress and a woman changing shapes (bodies?) in order to lead each other's lives (see chapter three). Does *Gautrek's Saga* describe ritual possession? If it doesn't, what else is it likely to be describing? A simpler explanation is that the *'possession'* involving the two men becoming Thor and Odin is actually ritual drama, which showed them taking the roles of the

---

370 Sturluson, *Heimskringla or the Lives of the Norse Kings*. 2004.
371 Wallis, *Shamans/Neo-Shamans*. 2003.
372 Ibid.
373 Grammaticus, *The Danish History of Saxo Grammaticus*. 2008.
374 Byock, *The Saga of the Volsungs*. 2004.
375 Palsson & Edwards, *Gautrek's Saga*. 1968.

gods. However, it depends drastically on our interpretation of ritual drama within antiquity, was deity possession intended as part of the ritual drama or was it simply drama? Does intense drama automatically have an element of altered states and even possession?

Working with the Norse deities should be a personal journey. Mythology and other people's understanding and knowledge will only tell you so much about your gods. Working with them, honouring them, communing with them, journeying to them, and listening to your instincts will tell you what you personally need to know and do in order to invoke them. Learning from other people, whether that is from primary or secondary sources will only take you so far. Yet, don't miss out on this stage. Before you work closely with a deity, read everything that you can about them; look at other people's art; find as many descriptions of them as you can. Below I have given a brief description and example invocation to the deities that I suggest working with using the rites from this book. I have only given short descriptions, and only to the four deities I work closest with. This is because there are many books available that focus on this area. Before invoking them, I would suggest that you learn more about them using the texts given at the beginning. Before I start invoking the deities, I like to intone their names. I end the invocations by explaining the reason for the invoking, whether that is simply to honour, to gain wisdom, or to actively work with the deity through possession or journeying.

FREYJA

Freyja is a Vanir goddess, famed for her beauty and sexuality. She is the goddess of seidr and witchcraft, and was said to have taught seidr to the Aesir gods.[376] She was also said to have been a priestess[377] and, linked to the Valkyries, to have had first choice of the battle slain who then came to live in her hall Folkvang[378]/Sessrumnir.[379] The myths that Freyja appears in show her as a strong, independent goddess. She sleeps with four dwarves in order

---

376 Faulkes, *Edda*. 1995.
377 Chisholm & Flowers (eds), *A Source-book of Seid*. 2002.
378 Larrington, *The Poetic Edda*. 1999.
379 Paxson, *Essential Asatru, Norse Paganism*. N.d.

to gain the necklace Brisingamen (showing her love of gold). In another story, she refuses to be used as bait and paraded in front of a giant which means that the god Thor has to dress as her instead.[380] Within the story of Ottar[381] we also see Freyja taking an initiatory role.

Invocation to Freyja

Freyja, Lady of the Vanir
Mistress of witchcraft and sorcery
Teacher of seidr to the Aesir
Golden lady of Brisingamen
Initiator of the golden boar

ODIN

Odin is a god of many names. He is the Allfather, or King of the Aesir gods and instrumental in much of the mythology.[382] He has two ravens, Hugin and Munin (thought and memory) who travel with him. Odin has only one eye, as he sacrificed the other one to Mimir's well. He gained the wisdom of the runes by sacrificing himself to himself, hanging from Yggdrasil for nine days and nine nights.[383] Odin is linked to seidr within *Lokasenna* where Loki accuses him of practising it. He was also said to be able to change his shape: *"his body would rest as in sleep or death but he became bird of beast, fish or worm, to travel instantly to far countries, in his own or other people's interest."* [384] *Ynglingasaga* tells us that Odin was also able to use seidr for prophecy.[385] When working with the Norse gods, I will often remember Odin, even if we are not specifically working with him during that rite, with three drops of wine or beer and the brief words *"three drops for Odin"*, or sometimes using the Swedish *"tre droppar till Odin"*.[386]

---

380 Crossley-Holland, *The Penguin Book of Norse Myths*. 1996.
381 Larrington, *The Poetic Edda*. 1999.
382 Faulkes, *Edda*. 1995.
383 Larrington, *The Poetic Edda*. 1999.
384 Fries, *Seidways*. 1996.
385 Chisholm & Flowers (eds), *A Source-book of Seid*. 2002.
386 This practice was given to me by Leila Wiberg

Invocation to Odin
To the Allfather I call out
Odin of the Aesir
Wise One Eye of Valhalla
Come Thought, Come Memory
To the High One I offer, three drops

HEL

Hel was the daughter of the union between Loki, the fire spirit, and Angrboda, the giantess.[387] From this union was also born the wolf Fenris (who later had to be fettered by the gods), and the Jormungard serpent (who was banished to the sea to encircle the world, biting his own tail). Hel, it can be argued in that case, is neither a goddess of the Aesir nor a goddess of the Vanir - and it can even be argued that she is not a goddess at all. However, when Odin banished her to the bottom world of Yggdrasil, she became queen of her realm, and therefore rightly takes her place within our rites as the goddess of the dead. Half of Hel's body is dead and takes the form of a corpse, while the other half is alive and a beautiful young woman.[388] When invoking Hel before journeying to her realm, we always ask for a safe entry and a safe return for those who are journeying there.

Invocation to Hel
Through the mists
We call out to the Queen of Helheim
Half flesh and beauty
Half decay and death
Queen of the dead, Helheim's mistress

FRIGGA

Frigga is Odin's wife and therefore the Queen of the Aesir.[389] She is known for her wisdom and also for her cunning. She spins the wool that the Norns weave into the

---

[387] Crossley-Holland, *The Penguin Book of Norse Myths*. 1996.
[388] Faulkes, *Edda*. 1995.
[389] Ibid.

web of wyrd and as such knows the fates of mankind,[390] but chooses not to share this knowledge with anyone. As Odin's wife her wisdom is shown through her ability to advise and guide him, but also for her ability to use her cunning to trick him, such as the time she made Odin choose her favourites rather than his to be the victors in battle. With her symbol of the keys, she is in charge of the household. Her fight to stop the death of her son Baldr shows her in her mother aspect, and she was often invoked during birth.

Invocation to Frigga
Mother of Baldr, we call to you
Frigga, weaver of fates
She who knows everything and says nothing
Wise Queen of the Aesir
With the keys of authority

BECOMING A HORSE

The term given in the contemporary pagan community to someone that is regularly possessed by deities (or a deity) is a horse.[391] This represents the idea that they are *'ridden'* by their gods, that their body is used and taken over by the deity. This theory originally comes from voudou communities whose Lwa possess the congregation as a part of rites.[392] Hrafnar are not the only Western contemporary pagan group experimenting with elements of possession and being ridden, it is an area that is slowly beginning to gain more and more popularity. Many of these groups use the ecstatic dance aspects of the rites of their inspiration, with lots of dancing, drumming, and trance. They also see the deity dancing and enjoying food and drink (and sometimes sexual relations) with other members of the community.[393]

Possession can be a very intense and exhilarating experience, however it can also be something that the horse does not remember (depending on the deity, the horse, and

---

390 Larrington, *The Poetic Edda*. 1995.
391 Filan & Kaldera, *Drawing Down the Spirits*. 2009.
392 Ibid.
393 Ibid.

the level of trance experienced).[394] You often hear people exclaiming that if you don't forget everything then you aren't really possessed[395] and even more often you hear debates as to whether or not someone was faking or delusional. Possession then, is clearly a contentious subject.

What is supposed to happen during a possession? Firstly, the level of cultural belief and context found within the Voudou traditions is not quite available within the Western possession traditions. Secondly, these are often mystery traditions which means that people are slowly and carefully trained and that the 'how to' knowledge is not published and often just passed on with word of mouth. Thirdly, many people believe that it is something that you are either 'wired' to do, or you aren't,[396] it isn't teachable.

'HORSING' THE NORSE

The first thing to consider when looking at incorporating possession of the Norse deities into your rites is whether the term 'horse's is the right one to use. It is a term commonly used within ecstatic possession, but is it really appropriate for the Norse? The horse in Northern mythology is associated most often with Sleipnir and as we can see from chapter one, with astral travel. A possessing deity comes to you. By using the term horse are we suggesting that these rites also contain other worldly journeying? If we don't use the term horse, what other words are available for us to use? What about Volva, Gythia, or Seidkona? All denote a priestess but what distinguishes between Odin's priestess who is possessed by him and Odin's priestess who honours him in other ways? Another term we could use could be house, or vessel, determining that the Volva contains the energy of the deity.

An important distinction between Norse possession and ecstatic possession is that the Norse deities will often possess in a slightly more subdued way. For example Filan and Kaldera in *Drawing Down the Spirits* suggest that the Norse deities don't dance and instead like to sit.[397] They

---

394 Wallis, *Shamans/Neo-Shamans*. 2003.
395 Filan & Kaldera, *Drawing Down the Spirits*. 2009.
396 Ibid.
397 Ibid.

are also less likely to fall about, being more in control of their host's bodies, and *"they also tend to stay a lot longer"*.[398] Is this because the rites of contemporary heathens lend themselves more to this kind of possession, or because of old the Norse gods were used to possessing in this way? With regards to them staying around longer, is this because contemporary Norse possession rites are less frequent and therefore there is more *'work'* to do when they occur?

LEVELS OF POSSESSION

As we have already encountered, one person's experience of possession can be very different to another's. There seems to be an ideal in contemporary paganism that a good possession is a forgotten possession, but is this really the case?

According to the *Old Testament*, true prophets spoke
> *"as mouthpieces of the spirit, but retained their free will. Total possession was condemned as being inappropriate."*[399]

Which of these beliefs is correct?

Umbanda ritualists believe that there are various levels of trance, and acknowledge that an individual's mind may affect the information gained.[400] When we consider this there are a few questions to ask. The first is whether the individual mind that is affecting the information is the conscious or the subconscious mind? The second is how much more likely it is that your mind will affect the information if you can remember proceedings than if you can't remember? Does total deity possession remove both the conscious and the subconscious minds? The Umbanda consider that sometimes it is possible to remember parts of the conversation.[401]

Filan and Kaldera give the definition of possession as:
> *"a possession experience is one in which the subject's identity is subsumed into Something Else;*

---

398 Filan & Kaldera, *Drawing Down the Spirits*. 2009.
399 Ibid.
400 Ibid.
401 Ibid.

the person loses control over speech and actions for a greater or lesser period of time."[402]

This suggests that the lack of control is the difference between being possessed or not. They go on to explain that there are rituals which require someone to draw some of the energy of the deity into them, but that the person is supposed to keep hold of their own memory and be responsible for their own actions. This is referred to as aspecting.[403] Blain suggests that whether or not someone remembers their trance seems to be related to their culture, for example, if culturally a *'proper'* trance is forgotten then so will theirs be, and if culturally trances and possessions are remembered then they will remember.[404] It seems that the answer to our question of whether a possession should or should not be remembered comes down to individual needs. Some people may remember, some may not, but some people are more likely to remember their dreams than others, or to be able to have lucid dreams. Is it more helpful to remember or not to remember?

There is also the element of how *'in control'* you are of proceedings. Whilst there are instances of people not being in control of what the possessing deity does or remember it, there are some that are and can. Filan and Kaldera tell us that:

> *"shamans have also traditionally used a technique... [that] allows the shaman to utilise the spirit's qualities for his own purpose while being completely in control of the situation."[405]*

We can remember from this that people are adaptable and that in the same way that people can be taught to remember and control their dreams, so can they learn to gain control within possession situations. My personal belief is that a deity possession is a two-way process. This is somewhat in opposition to Filan and Kaldera's approach (which is that you can't stop it but you can bargain for a change of time and place).[406] Certainly, if you work closely with a deity and have expected a lot from them, they may wish to suggest their payment; but it is possible to have a series of rules that you expect when working with deity, and

---

[402] Filan & Kaldera, *Drawing Down the Spirits*. 2009.
[403] Ibid.
[404] Blain, *Nine Worlds of Seid-Magic*. 2001
[405] Filan & Kaldera, *Drawing Down the Spirits*. 2009.
[406] Ibid.

they will also make their rules clear. A good deity relationship should be a partnership, not a manager and employee relation, and certainly not a slave and master relationship.

When it comes to the memory of possession and also to the memory of deep trance, my personal experience is that my memory has *'holes'* in. This can happen with both the deity possession work and also the seidr trances. There will be chunks of the conversation that I do remember, and chunks that I don't, but it is also very usual for me to have parts of the ritual that I didn't remember immediately afterwards coming back over the next few days. Sometimes there will be something that triggers this, for example *'yesterday you told me that....'* or the sight of something that reminds me. I find this to be very similar to dreams where I might be able to remember snatches of them in the morning, but the significant ones come back slowly throughout the day. The difference of course between a dream and a public trance state is that you have people on hand to help trigger those memories that are fading in and out.

Interestingly, during the trance I am often very aware of how conscious I still am, what I can see and hear; which words are forming around me, or are being formed by me. Very occasionally, an exchange might be confidential and there is an almost unwritten ideal that this is where my consciousness disappears, but it is never for very long and it is more like a lack of concentration for a moment rather than an extended period of blacking out. Part of the possession experience for me is the deep communication with the particular deity I am working with. This is a solid, strengthening process and feels very much like being surrounded by them, as though floating in water, rather than being pushed aside by them. The core of my energy remains the same, but it is supported by and surrounded by the deity energy.

POSSESSION RITE

This rite is given as an example of how you can use the techniques discussed at the beginning of this chapter in a ritual. I have chosen Freyja as the deity simply because I have worked with her extensively.

Many of the Norse deities seem to fit well within possession rites, it seems as though the rawness, and directness of the Norse deities fits well with this style of working. This main aim of this rite is for divination, although you can easily adapt it so that it becomes a rite for worship only, or you could also add a magic or seidr element to it that you could ask Freyja to bless as part of the rite.

When you are working with possession rites, remember that it isn't as simple as deciding upon a deity and expecting them to turn up to play. This isn't to say that sometimes you won't get results this way, but usually, it is far more beneficial to spend a period of time in deep contemplation and honour of that deity (for example a month or series of months), learning about their aspects, the myths associated with them, and any likes and dislikes. When it comes to knowing how they will move their energy into their host, it is likely to be something that becomes obvious to you (and every deity will be different). Similarly, it will be clear what they should be clothed in and what food and drink to offer them. If these questions are remaining, undertake journeys to meet with your deity and make sure you find out before you start.

* **Purify the space** *using your favoured method.*
* **Invoke personal protection** *appropriately. If you have a very strong link with your deity, it might be appropriate to ask them to make sure the rite goes well and that you emerge from it safe and healthy.*
* **Invocation to your deity**
* **State the intent of your rite**, *for example "I invoke Freyja to embody me so that we can gain advice and wisdom from her." Again, don't expect to get anything from the Norse entities without offering something in return. If you don't offer, don't be surprised to find that they take. Offerings can be in the form of food, drink, incense, time, or a task. You might want to ask your deity to stick around after the rite and party with you, but make sure you suggest a time limit.*

* **Bring the energy of your deity into the space**, *this works best by storytelling, and sharing appropriate imagery.*
* **Invoke the deity into the chosen host**, *every deity will have a different way that the energy enters their host. For example, Freyja enters quickly and we usually use a staff or stave, almost like a radio mast.*
* **Give the deity their costume**, *for example, a certain colour cloak or headdress, for Freyja a gold necklace and calfskin shoes are used.*
* **Give offering**, *find out through a series of journeys what they would like you to offer them (food, drink, music) before they start their work.*
* **The audience ask the deity questions**
* **Once you have got your answers,** *give any further promised offerings, (such as party time) and when you are finished, explain that the rite has ended.*
* **Ground the deity out of the host**, *you should have already worked out how to do this BEFORE you start the rite. For Freyja, her energy is visualised rising out of the staff.*
* **Thank the deity again and reiterate that the rite is over**
* **Ground and evaluate** *making note of any answers given that you want to remember.*

HIGH SEAT RITE TO ASGARD

> *This is a follow-on from the High Seat Rite that we found in chapter four. It uses the same techniques and ideals, but journeys to Asgard to meet and speak with the gods rather than a journey to Helheim to speak with the ancestors. I have included this rite here as an alternative to the possession rite for gaining wisdom and advice from the gods. The Seer here is in conversation with (and gaining her answers from) the gods in Asgard. You could also use the tree of Yggdrasil to transport spirits and ancestors up the tree to speak to the Seer, in the same way as the ancestors are transported down the tree to Helheim in the High Seat rite.*
>
> *Within this divination rite you are still gaining wisdom from the gods, although the information is channelled through your conscious: the Seer interacts with the gods, asks them questions, and relays the answers back, rather than the deities speaking through them as they do in the possession rites.*

* **Purification of the working space**, *an incense of frankincense, sage, and rosemary works well, you want the atmosphere nice and smoky.*
* **Invocation of the Disir circle** *(see chapter five)*
* **Invocation to Odin**, *to ask him to enter his realm.*
* **Invocation to Heimdall**, *for help through the gates. You might want to invoke specific deities here too, but be careful not to offend any that you forget. It is sometimes safer to keep it to a minimum for this reason!*
* **Raise energy for the rite** *(we do this via ecstatic dancing and drumming. With a bigger audience only the battery wildly dance and the audience sway and clap, but with a smaller group everybody dances.*
* **The drumming quietens and everyone sits in a circle**
* **All chant the Vardlokkur** *(we use "The Gate is open, the time has come, the seer's work, must be done' to a beat of four beats per second) During the Vardlokkur everyone sways and claps, while still seated.*
* **When the Seer is ready, they are given the staff and cloak and a pathworking to Asgard.** *The Master of*

Ceremonies keeps an eye on the Seer and decides when it is time to give them the pathworking. The drumming and the Vardlokkur chant quieten but never stop, not until the end of the rite. Only the Seer hears the pathworking: "The great tree Yggdrasil stands in the centre of the room. A doorway opens at its base and inside a tall, winding, spiral staircase leads as far as the eye can see. Take the staircase up through the tree, taking note of the worlds that you see on the way up. Ratatosk the squirrel runs up the outside of the tree."

* **The Seer is led around physically walking in a spiral** *"At the top of the tree you see the branches spread wide and a city stands across from you. Spreading across from the City is a rainbow bridge. The bridge is Bifrost and the city is Asgard. Heimdall the guardian stands between you and the bridge. You tell him what business you have in Asgard and he bids you to cross. Are you ready to make the journey into Asgard?"*

* **The Seer answers in the positive** *and the Master of Ceremonies physically leads them forward. At this point it works very well to have a horn blown before the Seer takes their first steps and a rattle shaken along with them as they walk.*

* **The Seer is sat on the High Seat** *and asked what they can see. They describe anything that is obvious straight away to them.*

* **The audience ask questions**

* **When the Seer is ready to go**, *they are stood up, called by their name, and taken back through the pathworking – bridge first, spiral staircase, and back down the tree.*

* **The Vardlokkurs and drumming stops**

* **The Seer is given food and drink and helped to ground**

* **The ancestors are thanked and asked to return through Yggdrasil**

* **Everyone grounds, and food and drink is shared**

* **Thank Heimdall and explain that the rite has ended**

* **Thank Odin and explain that the rite has ended**

* **Ground and evaluate, writing anything that seems important.**

CHAPTER EIGHT

SEIDR IN ANTIQUITY

This chapter looks at seidr and investigates some of the key questions that we have about the literature. It looks at the seidr of the past and asks the questions that interest contemporary practitioners, such as whether or not there is a link with the Sami, and just how strongly the Norse held onto the concept of seidr as ergi.

When considering these aspects, we must remember that much of what we know about seidr comes from very differing sources and that just as contemporary heathens are almost expected not to agree with each other, so were the seidr workers of the past. As Dubois so rightly states: *"It becomes clear that Nordic paganism was subject to extensive local variation and a fair degree of intercult rivalry"*[407] thus when we question we must be aware that there was no rule book, or even set of accepted practices, and therefore all we have are our best guesses based on the information that has survived.

DID THE NORSE BELIEVE IN SEIDR?

As we have seen, there are plenty of examples of seidr being written about within the Norse *Eddas* and *Sagas*. An assumption that we can build from this is that there was a culture of seidr, and also of prophecy within the Norse.

---

[407] Dubois, *Nordic Religions in the Viking Age.* 1999.

However, it is important to remember that many of the *Sagas*, although often based on true events, were written as literature and fiction. This allows for the authors to use artistic license both as entertainment and as plot devices, to hold the story together. It is also worth remembering that some of these *Sagas* would have started off as word of mouth, being written down at a later date. If we look at Snorri's *Edda*,[408] we understand that predominantly this is a work of fiction and ultimately of fantasy, telling stories of the gods of the past. Although an element of realism is evident within these tales, we do not know for sure which elements were widely accepted as believable and which were seen by its original audience as pure fantasy. This causes us significant confusion when we seek to answer the question of whether or not the Norse believed in seidr.

One thing that is resolutely missing from the *Sagas* and *Eddas* in their dealing with seidr is that there is no sense of disbelief from any of the characters; the ability of seidr to work is widely accepted. In *Laxdaela Saga*[409] for example, the household stays indoors and hides. In *Orkneyingasaga*,[410] the reappearance of the dead woman's body is not considered to be a dream or imagination. The layer of disbelief which you often find within literature that deals with comparable supernatural experiences (for example Victorian ghost stories) is not there. No walking corpses are explained away as a *'crumb of cheese*[411] on an upset stomach, no prophecy is ignored or dismissed. Was this because they were widely accepted phenomena or was this because the opposite was true and it was understood that it was so ridiculous that of course it was fiction? Interestingly, many of the Classical Greek texts have similar motifs, and there is also a lack of question and disbelief in these. The fantasy in the *Odyssey*,[412] for example, is accepted by the characters in the story. The *Odyssey* deals with myths that were widely known and understood culturally by the Greeks which may have been why in this example the questions were not asked. Were the *Sagas* and *Eddas* such popular, well known tales that the supernatural elements were not expected to be explained?

---

408 Faulkes, *Edda*. 1995.
409 Magnusson et al., *Laxdaela Saga*. 1975.
410 None, *Orkneyinga Saga*. 2004.
411 Dickens, *The Christmas Books*. 2007.
412 Homer, *The Odyssey*. 2003.

We have an understanding within academia that the Norse believed in their gods and, although much of the literature has come from a time when Christianisation was in process, I believe that this clearly comes across in the texts. The burial customs were obviously followed, with the examples of walking corpses happening when they were not. How much of the scary aspects of the stories were borrowed from the Classical or became more prominent post-Christianisation? The concepts of hugr and fylgia discussed earlier in the book are presented in the literature as being widely acknowledged beliefs.[413] Is a belief in seidr really only a step removed from this?

The other question we should ask when looking at the role of seidr within the *Sagas* was whether or not it was a plot device. Prophecies play a large part in the stories, as precursors to show the reader what is happening and to set the scene. Similarly, sorcery and magical seidr explain plot twists and turns and play an important role in the progression of the storylines.

How much of the *Sagas* were true and how much were fiction? Many of the *Sagas* involve historical figures and events and their focus seems to be on remembering and honouring the ancestors. Therefore, the assumption is that they were written to be truthful. Yet some elements such as the seidr, when looked at contemporarily, lead us to believe that they were fiction because through contemporary eyes the magical elements look like they could be fairy story or allegorical. It is impossible for us to have the answers; therefore we can only form ideas and opinions. I will move on from this question with the information that, at school, I was taught that the Vikings did not reach America. The *Vinland Sagas*, although pretty clear on this subject, were taught to me as mythology and as impossible to be true. Yet archaeological evidence[414] has uncovered Viking settlements in Canada and North America, thus backing up the *Vinland Sagas*.

ON ERGI

A chapter on the Norse Seer and on seidr and the volva would not be complete without stepping into the subject of

---

[413] Strömbäck et al., *Sejd.* 2000.
[414] Magnusson et al., *The Vikings.* 2008.

'ergi'. Within the literature, seidr was the realm of women and therefore men who practiced seidr were described as either *ergi* or *argr*. This has been a huge area of discussion for modern heathen practitioners, especially those who are male.[415] Those interested in the concept of ergi are strongly recommended to read Jenny Blain's *Nine Worlds of Seid Magic* which discusses ergi in academic detail. In the interest of not repeating what has already been explored very well, I hope that I can add to and build on the work that Blain has already started in this area.

Ergi is often translated loosely as unmanly[416] or acting as a woman;[417] a step further than this then is to use the term homosexual. The general consensus (and I would suggest, rightly) seems to be that in today's practice, there is no reason why men should not practice seidr or should feel that seidr makes them less of a man in any way. This said, Blain[418] points out that a high proportion of the men practising seidr (especially those who take on the role of the volva on the high seat) are gay.

Diana Paxson tells us that *"the majority of those who practice seidh in the Sagas are female. The strong feminine tradition makes this form of shamanism especially interesting to women."*[419] Men who practiced seidr include Ragnvald, the son of Harald Fairhair[420] in *Heimskingla* and Kotkel in *Laxdaela Saga*.[421] Ragnvald was thought to have brought great shame on his family and at the request of his father was shut indoors and the building burnt with him (and those men who practiced seidr with him) inside. The strength of the feminine tradition associated with seidr, as Paxson says, makes it clearly a tradition that women are likely to be attracted to, but also cements it as being something for women within the tradition of heathenry (with its Viking and sword-wielding heroes that could be said to naturally attract men).

The two chapters in *Lokasenna* that use the term argr are translated by Caroline Larrington as follows:

---

415 Blain, *Nine Worlds of Seid-Magic*. 2001.
416 Ibid.
417 Jochens, *Women in Old Norse Society*. 1998.
418 Blain, *Nine Worlds of Seid-Magic*. 2001.
419 Paxson, *The Return of the Volva*. 1993.
420 Sturluson, *Heimskringla*. 2004.
421 Magnusson et al., *Laxdaela Saga*. 1975.

Odin to Loki
"yet eight winters you were, beneath the earth,
A woman milking cows,
And there you bore children,
And that I thought the hallmark of a pervert"[422]

Loki to Odin
"but you once practiced seid on Samsey,
And you beat on a drum as witches do,
In the likeness of a wizard you journeyed among
mankind,
And that I thought the hallmark of a pervert."[423]

Argr is translated as being *'a pervert'* linking in with the theory that *ergi* and *argr* are about being sexually female rather than just acting in a feminine way. The mythology that *Lokasenna* is referring to is Odin's shape shifting (Jan Fries goes further and suggests this refers to Odin transforming himself into a woman)[424]. Loki is referred to as argr because he gives birth to the horse Sleipnir after turning into a mare, becoming pregnant and gestating and giving birth.[425] The translations suggest that the term ergi when directed at men practising seidr, was given as an insult. Blain questions this,[426] and also questions whether we are wearing too much of a modern viewpoint when we refer to ergi as being homosexual, considering that homosexuality as a concept is (in historical terms) recent. Blain also suggests that this is a Western concept that isn't necessarily viewed in the same way within indigenous cultures.[427]

In looking at the unmanly aspect of seidr, Blain suggests that seidr was effeminising because it included receptive activities, for example, channelling energies, or becoming a *'vessel'*. Blain also points out that a person in a trance state (and especially the deep trance state that seidr requires) becomes very vulnerable and therefore reliant on the other people around them. Is this, therefore, unmanly? If we look further into the receptive (and

---

422 Larrington, *The Poetic Edda*. 1999.
423 Ibid.
424 Fries, *Seidways*. 1996.
425 Crossley-Holland, *The Penguin Book of Norse Myths*. 1996.
426 Blain, *Nine Worlds of Seid-Magic*. 2001.
427 Ibid.

especially sexually receptive) qualities that could be associated with seidr, we see that to the Norse, to be sexually passive was a female quality and to be sexually active was a male quality.[428] In fact, interestingly, the term ergi has also been applied to women. In this instance, a women who *'took the initiative sexually'* therefore becoming sexually active rather than sexually passive. Does this mean that ergi is both *'a woman acting as a man'* and *'a man acting as a woman'*?[429] The concept of men being sexually active and women being sexually passive was switched after Christian influence came into play and the emphasis became towards who was to blame for sexual encounters. Post-Christianity the woman became seen as the active seducer and the man was given a more passive role.[430]

Bringing us back to the association of ergi with homosexuality, I am left with the feeling that simply being *'unmanly'* or indeed *'unfeminine'* doesn't automatically equal homosexuality. Further investigation into whether the Norse had anything like a concept of homosexuality brought me to Jenny Jochen's discussion on gender. Jochens identifies two specific terms *sordit* and *sordinn*. Sordit refers to the act of penetration (to take the active role in sex), and sordinn refers to the act of being penetrated (to take the passive role in sex). Ergi seems instead to refer to who takes the initiative rather than to who takes the role of penetration. If the reason male seidr practitioners were referred to as ergi or argr was solely down to homosexuality, then would *sordinn* not be a more appropriate term?

The terminology used in *Lokasenna* was argr. Blain suggests that this is becoming sexually female, or displaying non masculine behaviour.[431] Jochens suggested that it is linked to the word *ragr* which is used to refer to someone who is effeminate. Jan Fries looks at how the word has developed into the word *arg* which he gives as meaning something like evil in German and translating as sinful or lustful in Old Swedish.[432] Blain has discovered the term argi being used in Scotland. Parts of Scotland were settled by the Norse and the rich Scottish heritage in parts

---

428 Jochens, *Women in Old Norse Society*. 1998.
429 Ibid.
430 Ibid.
431 Blain, *Nine Worlds of Seid-Magic*. 2001.
432 Fries, *Seidways*. 1996.

betrays this. A well-known Norse saga was written about the Orkney Islands.[433] Blain gives an example of the way that the term argi is used in Scotland which looks as though it is being used to refer to cowardice, or at least to someone who was seen to shy away from or refuse to use violence in dealing with a situation where others would have felt it appropriate.[434] Perhaps a southern British equivalent would be to refer to someone as being 'soft' in a similar situation. Certainly, being 'soft' could easily amount to being unmanly but doesn't automatically refer to homosexuality.

Argi used in Scotland to refer to cowardice and to someone 'holding back violence'.[435]

Let's consider that cowardice and 'holding back violence' can refer to two separate instances. Cowardice suggests running away from a situation or indeed it can also refer to letting someone else fight your battles or choosing stronger weapons than your opponent. Not fighting fairly. Is seidr cowardly? If we look at instances of seidr where it is used to trick opponents into coming out into the open,[436] or to appear to someone while they are sleeping (and therefore in a more vulnerable situation) then we can indeed wonder whether the term ergi was used simply because seidr wasn't as honourable or as manly as challenging an enemy to a fair fight. Does 'holding back violence' equal cowardice necessarily? Certainly, Kotkel and his family in Laxdaela Saga show "a reluctance to fight their battles in the open".[437] To the Viking world where combat and the warrior were championed, it is understandable that men who were using seidr and mind tricks to fight were seen as ergi and unnatural. We can also consider whether, on reflection, it could be said that to hold back violence was to show compassion. From a modern western viewpoint you could argue that this is a braver thing to do, but to the Norse, was compassion a feminine attribute?

There was certainly a distinction within Norse society between what was appropriate behaviour for men and women. Saxo Grammaticus introduces us to the priests of

---

[433] None, Orkneyinga Saga.
[434] Blain, Nine Worlds of Seid-Magic. 2001.
[435] Ibid.
[436] Magnusson et al., Laxdaela Saga. 1975.
[437] Dubois, Nordic Religions in the Viking Age. 1999.

Freyr in Uppsala in Sweden (the changing ones)[438] who became 'wives' of the God Freyr. The changing ones wore dresses fringed with bells and had gestures which were considered to be feminine. Within this source it is also suggested that the sound of the bells themselves was even considered to be feminine. The distinction between men and women's roles was also in place when it came to the division of labour. Men worked outdoors, women worked indoors. Women had a great deal of responsibility within the home and were responsible for most of what happened inside it. A man's place was out of doors when it came to work.[439] Men and women even had different roles when it came to entertaining, with Jochens highlighting that the storyteller was a male role, and that the female equivalent was possibly the prophetess.[440] Is it the case, however, that those involved in mysticism didn't fit neatly into these ideals (whether male or female)? Blain points out that the shaman of a society can straddle both sexes and therefore becomes a third sex.[441]

While we consider what 'men's work' is and what 'women's work' is, we can also look at this interesting quote from Jacqueline Simpson:

> "An interesting group of Icelandic folktales runs counter to gender stereotyping in a different way, showing a wife who protects her husband from supernatural danger by her superior psychic awareness and her knowledge of correct magical procedures."[442]

This leads us to speculate whether these were folktales that were bucking the trend in belief of what women's work was within the Norse (even if that concept is different from that of our own ideals). Was it a woman's role to protect her family from supernatural danger? Bearing in mind that a man's role was to protect from intruders attempting to enter the home (therefore outside), was it a woman's role to protect from psychic and supernatural intruders? Looking for more hints that this might have been the case, I found this example:

---

438 Grammaticus, *The Danish History of Saxo Grammaticus*. 2008.
439 Jochens, *Women in Old Norse Society*. 1999.
440 Ibid.
441 Blain, *Nine Worlds of Seid-Magic*. 2001.
442 Simpson, *Be Bold, but not too Bold*. 1991.

> *"A common topos in the narratives is the magical*
> *coats and shirts provided by female magicians to*
> *protect their male favourites."*[443]

Although we absolutely have to remember that making clothes was the responsibility of women, the idea that magical clothes were made for the task of protecting is something worth thinking more about. Jochens also says that women were also considered to be good at recollection of past events, which might help to explain why prophets, responsible to future events, were female.[444]

When we consider whether magic and supernatural protection was the role of women we need to remember that galdr and rune magic was often considered to be male, but also that there exist a number of accounts of male seidr practitioners. If we can look at related cultural practices we don't see that much of a pattern forming. The Greek oracles and sybils were female,[445] yet the Sami and Siberian shamans were more likely to be male.[446] Within the UK history, folk belief has given the witch figure over to the feminine, but some of the most well remembered cunning folk were men.[447] Phyllis Mack[448] in her investigation of the English Civil War prophets tells us that during this time prophecy was considered to be something that was done by women.

> *"Women were suited to be prophets because of their*
> *essence, which was irrational, emotional, and*
> *unusually receptive to outside influences."*[449]

This brings me to the concept of 'women's intuition' - is there really a case for it? Does childbirth really make someone more likely to be connected to the supernatural and to 'the other'? The above quote is specifically talking about a time when women were not expected to speak out publicly, and especially were not expected to speak out about politics. A level of irrationality and possible insanity allowed a woman to lecture and speak out politically in a way that would have been dangerous at that time. A woman's position within Norse society was stronger,

---

[443] Jochens, *Women in Old Norse Society.* 1998.
[444] Ibid.
[445] See chapter three
[446] Hutton, *The Shamans of Siberia.* 1993.
[447] Davies, *Cunning-folk.* 2003.
[448] Mack, *Women as Prophets during the English Civil War.* 1982.
[449] Ibid.

therefore it would not have been necessary to hide opinions behind mental instability. Yet even with this, is there enough evidence to suggest that women were considered better at protecting their families supernaturally, with men being better at protecting their families spiritually?

The concept of ergi is one that has enjoyed a great deal of consideration and debate and no doubt this will continue. Is it sufficient enough for us, after examining the concept, to say that the gender divisions and stereotyping from Norse society are significantly different from that within our own societies, and therefore the concept of ergi and seidr being the domain of the female is not relevant to the modern practice of seidr? Having said this, can it also be considered that the concept of ergi found within the literature of the North has been over-emphasised and overplayed by contemporary heathens? Certainly, when we begin to look into the examples of seidr, we find that there are plenty of examples of men working seidr. Jochens tells us that:

> *"on the whole, male and female magicians performed the same acts, although some gender distribution is noticeable when women wove shirts while men prepared swords"*[450]

This quote is specifically referring to the sorcery aspects of seidr. Interestingly, it seems that within prophecy, a greater number of women are described than men. The *Orkneyingasaga*[451] does give an example of a male prophesising, but does this reflect the role that men had within Scottish prophecy more than the role that men had within prophesising in mainland Scandinavia?

In concluding, I throw open the understanding that gender roles have been carefully considered, studied, and revisited often within the last century, and this is echoed within contemporary paganism. New theories and research are continually evaluating and re-evaluating what it means to be male or female, and the pendulum swings towards whether or not it makes a difference to abilities, skills, and roles within families. Certainly, the most important message that has come out from all of the consideration is that people are individuals and therefore individuals can be proficient in certain skills and not so proficient in others

---

[450] Jochens, *Old Norse Images of Women*. 1998.
[451] None, *Orkneyinga Saga*. 2004.

whatever their gender may be. After all, gender itself is also individual and is not as simple as simply male and female. Ergi, therefore, is a term that is not used within my own practice. All genders access all roles.

SAMI BORROWING WITHIN THE NORSE

As we have seen in many of the chapters so far, there seems to be a strong link between seidr and the shamanistic traditions of their northern neighbours the Sami, the Finns,[452] and the Siberians. Many of those who practiced seidr (and sometimes the seidr itself) were described as being foreign in some way, with many of these descriptions using the terms 'Finn' and 'Lapp'. There is certainly a theory that suggests that the seidr comes from these areas. The link between the Sami and seidr has been made by various different people, perhaps most notably Dubois[453] and Stromback.[454] O Donoghue believes that:

"It is only natural that Norse mythology might have also been influenced by the mythology and religion of the neighbours of the Norse: the hunter-gatherer Finns, and the present-day Northern Siberian Sami people, whose shamanistic beliefs still echo Norse traditions: shape shifting (assuming animal form) and perhaps, most strikingly, a world tree, stretching up to the heavens, balancing the whole world around its central axis."[455]

More often than not the *Sagas* refer to 'the Finns', as the source of training and inspiration. Blain believes that this probably refers to the Sami.[456] There is a huge likelihood of this, however, the Finns were a separate tribe to the Sami and they also had their own shamanistic traditions.[457]

There is clear evidence to show a relationship between seidr magic and Finnish sorcery.[458] Jan Fries tells us that *"People used to travel to Finnmark to buy spells and*

---

[452] Fries, *Seidways*. 1996.
[453] Dubois, *Nordic Religions in the Viking Age*. 1999.
[454] Strömbäck et al., *Sejd*. 2000.
[455] O'Donoghue, *From Asgard to Valhalla*. 2008.
[456] Blain, *Nine Worlds of Seid-Magic*. 2001.
[457] Dubois, *Nordic Religions in the Viking Age*. 1999.
[458] Fries, *Seidways*. 1996.

talismans"[459] whilst Blain points out that *"The seeresses often are said to have been trained by 'the Finns' which probably refers to the nomadic Sami"*.[460] The *Greenland Saga* clearly suggests that Haldis remembers the right Vardlokkurs because she has a Finnish foster mother, designating a link between Finland and spirit songs.[461] In *Ynglingasaga*, Vanlandi wishes to go to Finland, but his friends suggested that this was caused by Finnish magic.[462] We have already discussed that many of the seidr practitioners are described as being foreigners,[463] but as Blain shows us, although many of these are said to be Finns or Lapps, some of these foreigners with magical abilities are said to be from the Hebrides.[464] As discussed in chapter two, one of the links with the Finnish culture seems to be the seidhjallr,[465] as well as the staff/world tree. In *Vatnsdoela Saga* a woman invited to prophesise at a feast was described as being Finnish/Sami.[466]

Between the Lapp shamanism and seidr there are some striking similarities, for example the ecstatic sleep or trance states and also the magic songs. The seidhjallr can also be said to have its roots within the Finnish traditions as they also had the raised platform, from which they worked their magic. Interestingly, similarities also come between the Sami and Snorri's idea of the worlds of the dead with Sami belief having a goddess ruling their place of the dead, and a concept of a place where the wicked dead went (which was ruled over by a god).[467]

The trade routes did not stop with the Sami and the Finnish peoples, the Norse were also trading with (and therefore aware of) the religious beliefs of Russia and Siberia. Ellis Davidson tells us that:

> *"One important road for such influences might be south westwards from the lands of the Lapps; another that north westwards from the Norse settlements in Russia. We know that there was*

---

[459] Fries, *Seidways*. 1996.
[460] Blain, *Nine Worlds of Seid-Magic*. 2001.
[461] Jones, *Erik the Red and Other Icelandic Sagas*. 1961.
[462] Sturluson, *Heimskringla or the Lives of the Norse Kings*. 2004.
[463] Dubois, *Nordic Religions in the Viking Age*. 1999.
[464] Blain, *Nine Worlds of Seid-Magic*. 2001.
[465] Ibid.
[466] Dubois, *Nordic Religions in the Viking Age*. 1999.
[467] Ibid.

considerable movement along both in the heathen period.[468]

This allows us to consider that not only could the Norse have had access to the magic and shamanistic practices of Finland, it is also very possible for them to have had access to some of the Siberian shaman practices.

The *Poetic Edda* (through Grimnir's sayings) gives us a description of something that Carolyne Larrington suggests might recall shamanic rituals. Within *Grimnir's Sayings*, King Geirrod is tricked by Frigga into thinking that the guise Odin is travelling in (Grimnir) is going to cause him problems and that he needs to torture him. King Geirrod uses torture of starvation and lack of water and fire, through which Odin speaks words of wisdom to Frigga's favourite. Larrington suggests that this torture to create wisdom is hinting at the knowledge of shamanic practices and that it follows similar practice by the Finns at that time.[469]

A question we can ask is at what point the borrowing happened. Certainly, the link between sorcery and Finland seems fully developed during the period when the *Sagas* were written. However, there are similarities between many of the northern shamanistic tribes and their practice. A vast proportion of these tribes were nomadic which means it is likely that they interacted. Certainly, there was a vast amount of trade between them by the time the *Sagas* were written.[470] At what point did the borrowing occur, and who borrowed from whom? Jenny Blain believes that there is more to the development of seidr than simply a Sami loan[471] and clearly this must be the case, but the similarities between particularly the seidhjallr, the staff, the shape shifting and the vardlokkurs can't be ignored. Was it the case that the north had shamanistic traditions that were slowly forgotten as the north became Christianised and that these were borrowed and traded among the northern nomadic tribes?

> *"Since the spirits of dead shamans were thought to be more powerful than living ones, the land of the dead came to be regarded as a store-house of shamanic wisdom. Hence the visits of Vainamoinen*

[468] Ellis, *The Road to Hel.* 1943.
[469] Larrington, *The Poetic Edda.* 1999.
[470] Dubois, *Nordic Religions in the Viking Age.* 1999.
[471] Blain, *Nine Worlds of Seid-Magic.* 2001.

in the Kalevala to Tuonela (the land of the dead) and to the grave of the song giant Vipunen, in order to obtain his three lost words of master magic.[472]

It is important to remember that Christianisation came to different parts of the north at different times and this reflects in the amount of shamanistic traditions that they held onto and lost at different times. Christianity was very much known within the Scandinavia of the *Sagas*, although it is clear that many people still followed the older religion and that although some of the practices had been forgotten, many still existed. Shamanic beliefs and practices continued in the far North way beyond Christianisation, Palsson describes stories from the fourteenth century which talks of people being taught witchcraft,[473] and as late as 1928 Francis Jenkins Olcott recorded the Lapps still using magic incantations that combined the traditional beliefs with Christianity.

In considering the evidence found, it is clear that the Norse people were not ignorant of their neighbours, nor did they have a lack of understanding and interest in other religions. Although the landscape and climate meant that travel across the north might not have been as easy as travel elsewhere on the globe, the tribes in this area did trade goods and ideas. It is clear also that there was no fear or distrust in outside religions, Christianity was not opposed and in many of the Northern areas the Christian deities were simply acknowledged and added to the already integrated pantheons. For example, Larrington tells us that two of the favourites in Finland were Vainamoinen and the Virgin Mary.[474] It seems likely then that seidr, whilst being described as being foreign and having elements of similarity with the Northern tribes, could include elements borrowed from them.

For our contemporary practice, this link is incredibly beneficial. Where elements suggesting how the practices were actually implemented are missing, it is possible to look over to Scandinavia's neighbours to help fill in the gaps. Whether or not these ideas and practices would have been the ones used within the seidr traditions, we can never know, but if there are areas that we need to borrow from in

---

[472] Bonser, *The Magic of the Finns*. 1924.
[473] Palsson, *Voluspa*. 1996.
[474] Larrington, *The Poetic Edda*. 1999.

order to complete our contemporary practice, then these Northern shamanistic tribes are a very good place to investigate.

BORROWING FROM THE CLASSICAL WORLD

Although it can be said that many of the themes in this book could have been borrowed from the Sami and Finnish people, it has also been suggested that many of the supernatural motifs from the *Sagas* and *Eddas* could have been influenced by the Classical World.[475] It is well documented that the Norse trade routes brought them access to (and later conversion to) Christianity, but it also had the ability to bring them ideas, mythology, and literature from Greece and Rome. Dubois[476] reminds us that Latin was understood and used by many of the Norse traders, and that, through Latin, the Norse *"became acquainted with the major ideas of the Classical and Christian world."*[477]

In chapter one, we looked at the Volva and the poem Voluspa. Strong comparisons can be made between the Volva in Voluspa and the sybils of the classical world. Dronke, in *Myths and Fiction in Early Norse Lands* explains that:

> *"In 1879 the theologian AC Bang argued that Voluspa was a 'Norse Christian sibylline oracle: a Norse Christian poet's imitation of the sibylline texts... by following the Norse poem step by step, at virtually every point he had found parallels with the Greek oracles."*[478]

Was Voluspa inspired by Classical oracles? Was Snorri's prophetess inspired by classical oracles? Dronke believes that this is not the case, explaining that Norse seers worked through visions and in the majority of cases, the Hellenic oracles did not.

The similarities between the Norse and Classical prophets do not end with Voluspa, however. The pythonesses of the Classical world prophesised from platforms, which evokes memories of the seidhjallr;

---

[475] Dronke, *Myth and Fiction in Early Norse Lands*. 1996.
[476] Dubois, *Nordic Religions in the Viking Age*. 1999.
[477] Ibid.
[478] Dronke, *Myth and Fiction in Early Norse Lands*. 1996.

however, the raised platform can also be found in the neighbouring shamanistic tribes. Jochens points out that the role of the Norse prophet was also distinctly different from that of the Classical based on the amount of independence that they had:

> *"Germanic women enjoyed a monopoly over intuitive or spontaneous prediction, in contrast to the Near Eastern and Greek sibyls whose manic utterances required interpretation from male priests. Germanic priestess' spoke rationally and of their own volition."*[479]

This reflects the difference in independence that Norse women had in relation to Hellenic women however, so may be due to cultural not oracular aspects.

Evidence of borrowing ideas from the Classical world can also be found in other areas of the Norse literature. For example, in chapter five, we looked at the concepts of walking corpses and funeral customs. The concept of wandering dead and walking corpses is rife in Classical literature[480] with lack of correct burial practices only being one reason for the dead to rise. When Odin raises the Seer from the dead, we see a concept in the Norse of sorcerers being able to reanimate corpses. The Classical world had a very similar concept to this with many spells and incantations to animate corpses being found in the literature.[481] The idea of the dead taking the ferry to the otherworld that is so well-known within contemporary understanding of Greek antiquity also began to show up within the Norse.[482]

We can see, then, that some of the Classical concepts did make their way across to Scandinavia. When it comes to how much of the ideas found in seidr were borrowed from the Classical world, the question is: How much of the similarities between the Norse and the Classical prophets are coincidental? And did some of these ideas and concepts appear within Norse literature and society before they had access to the Classical literature? Lastly, how many of these ideas and concepts could also have been borrowed from elsewhere?

---

[479] Jochens, *Old Norse Images of Women*. 1996.
[480] Ogden, *Greek and Roman Necromancy*. 2004.
[481] Ibid.
[482] Dubois, *Nordic Religions in the Viking Age*. 1999.

The themes found within the Classical and the Norse concepts of prophecy and sorcery, although startlingly similar, are motifs that are also found in other cultures across the world. Is it likely, therefore, that although some of the literature (especially the later examples, such as *Volsungasaga*) might have borrowed from the Classical, the concepts of the Volva and the Seer's prophesies existed within Norse culture already?

CHAPTER NINE

CONTEMPORARY SEIDR

In this chapter we examine some of the questions that arise within the modern practice of seidr. We look at the specifics of trance states, links between contemporary seidr and mediumship and contemporary shamanism, as well as examining the shaking trance that Jan Fries associates with seidr.

WHERE DOES THE INFORMATION COME FROM?

Looking at the prophesising that happens within the contemporary seidr rites that we have described and explored, there are likely to be questions arising around the information gleaned. How useful is it? Where does it come from? How much should we trust it? In chapter eight we looked at whether or not the Norse believed in seidr and prophecy, and partly this chapter starts with the question of how much we believe our own prophecies, and if we believe that we should, what makes these prophecies different to those that come without the extensive rituals?

In the rites, the information is usually given in response to a question. The answers, in my experience, differ enormously from seer to seer, and often also from question to question. Some answers might come in riddles, using imagery and codes that the questioner will need to consider and interpret. Some, on the other hand, are scarily clear and blunt. Sometimes a question will be ignored and

179

the seer instead will focus on an unasked question, possible one that the questioner had forming in their head but decided not to ask.

In the High Seat Rite the intention is that the Seer journeys to Helheim in order to converse with spirits. In this instance then, do the spirits provide the answers? Jordsvin, a seidr practitioner is quoted by Blain as saying:

> *"I expect most of this is coming from the dead people, because this is where I go"*[483]

This explanation requires you to believe in the existence of spirits and the seer's ability to interact with them. What then allows a seer to interact with spirits during this rite where they are not necessarily able to interact with them at other times? A possible answer to this question is the simple use of the altered state of consciousness that allows the seer to interact in a different way to the way they interact in the mundane world. Is this enough? Various mythologies (for example Odysseus' journey to the Underworld) suggest that in order to interact with the spirit world a type of spiritual or metaphoric death needs to occur. This is backed up by Stuart A Harris Logan in the below quote from his book *Singing with Blackbirds*:

> *"In some cultures, trance is seen to be a kind of death. When the shaman enters an ecstatic state, he is considered to belong to the spirit world, no longer a part of material reality. When the shaman returns, he is thought to have transcended death."*[484]

Is the trance state itself enough of a metaphoric death then to induce the communication with spirit? How do the spirits communicate this information? Many Seers will receive the information in picture or metaphoric form, giving the imagery that they see to their questioner. I find personally that, during my trance state, I see the spirits stepping forward in Helheim and giving verbal answers to the queries. Occasionally images and ideas will also formulate, but the verbal exchange forms the majority. This probably says more about my need for anthropomorphism than it does about what is the best way to receive visions, and it is important to remember that it is likely to be different for everyone.

---

[483] Blain, *Nine Worlds of Seid-Magic*. 2001.
[484] Harris-Logan, *Singing with Blackbirds*. 2006.

Although the information can sometimes be in code or metaphoric form, a distinct difference between seidr and other forms of prophecy is exactly what we found in chapter eight, when looking at the differences between seidr and Classical prophecy: *"Her words were understood directly by her clients without mediating officials."*[485] The meaning of the prophecy may not be clear to the rest of the audience, but more often than not it is relevant and understood by the questioner. Often all of the prophecy might not become clear for many years, but even with this, there are usually elements that make sense immediately, even just to the questioner. The most remarkable of messages are those where the Seer is unaware of information that would allow them to understand what they are explaining, especially where very often, the seer has not met with the questioner before. Jordsvin, again to Blain, continues:

> *"I get people coming up to me after these seidr sessions when I'm stuffing my face and they will say oh you said... and I'll say I wonder what that means and they'll say, well it meant this. I did not know this."*[486]

Perhaps considering what the information is and where it comes from is not as important as considering and evaluating how useful that information was to the questioner and whether it helped them within their lives. Like many other forms of divination, such as Tarot or Astrology, perhaps it is impossible to fully decide how and why it works. We could even consider whether, in fact, it is illusion and chance that allows the message to be helpful. However, if the questioner leaves with information that helps them, even if it is just food for thought and a new angle on a problem, seidr for prophecy has been beneficial.

ENERGY

Many of the rites listed in this book refer to energy-raising and consciousness changing. The concept of 'energy' is an interesting one. Many neo pagan traditions (for example Wicca and Druidry) have an understanding that, in order to create changes or make things happen, you need to have a push of 'energy'. This is echoed within

---

485 Jochens, *Old Norse Images of Women.* 1996.
486 Blain, *Nine Worlds of Seid-Magic.* 2001.

Lindquist's description of Yggdrasil's rites, she explains that the ecstatic dancing and drumming *'builds energy.*[487] This is also something that can be found within the spiritualist tradition, which asks that energy is raised through hymns being sung in order to allow the spirits to manifest. Although this seems to have become an accepted idea within contemporary paganism, if we look at it from an outsider perspective, it loses a little of its understanding. What is energy? Why do we need it? How can singing or dancing affect changes? How can it be possible to heal the earth by singing?

From my basic school understanding of Physics, I am aware that energy cannot be created or destroyed, but that it can be changed and become something else. Considering energy in this way, it doesn't seem such a huge leap of faith to accept that energy can be harnessed and shaped in order to achieve other things. Depending on how we think of spirits and deities, the amount of energy we think we need to give them in order for them to exist and manifest changes. The Norse believed that speaking about and remembering their ancestors kept them alive. Are the gods alive because we remember them and tell their stories? Or are they something bigger and stronger with the ability to control and shape our lives and destinies? Are they able to have this impact because, like huge batteries, they absorb and release the energy given by worship?

Antiquity, if we look to the Greek philosophers, threw up the same kinds of questions. Although the Classical world did not have the concept of batteries and electricity, they did have an understanding of energy and life force. Even the most basic of human understanding allows us to see the difference between living and dead, and of strength and ability coming from eating that which has lived. In book eleven of the *Odyssey*, Odysseus uses the blood of cattle in order to create a gateway to the underworld and manifest it on a deserted island.[488] By using the life energy of the cattle, he is able to manifest. Is this a similar concept to us using the kinetic and sound energy of dancing and chanting the Vardlokkurs to enact the final push that allows the seer to pass through the gates of fire and ice and into the Helheim? In the *Greenland Saga*, Thorbjorg eats the hearts

---

[487] Lindquist, *Shamanic Performances on the Urban Scene.* 1997.
[488] Homer, *The Odyssey.* 2003.

of one of each animal that lives on the farmstead.[489] Is this because the heart holds the most life force and Thorbjorg needs this energy in order to prophesise? Another theory could be that in order to commune with the spirits of the land, she needed to have understanding and a link to them, and the consuming of the hearts was able to give her this. Robert J Wallis likens this to Celtic Seers eating vast quantities of meat before they went into trance states:[490]

> *"the consumption of excessive quantities of carnivore liver induced hypervitaminosis A, with the altered consciousness associated symptoms of migraine, drowsiness, diplopia, nausea, and vomiting."*[491]

Was Thorbjorg's consumption of the hearts therefore something that, instead of bringing spiritual assistance, helped to induce physical symptoms which allowed her to prophesise?

The concept of gaining wisdom through eating the heart of an animal is echoed within *Volsungasaga*, where Sigurd ate the heart of Fafnir the dragon and through doing so gained wisdom that allowed him to understand what the birds were saying. We could look at this as Sigurd gaining the ability to prophesise via a kind of bird augury. Similarly, we can link it straight back to Thorbjorg and suggest that, as the dragon could understand what the birds were saying, Sigurd, on eating his heart, was also able to. Did Thorbjorg, through eating the hearts of the animals, gain the ability to understand the language of the animals which helped her to prophesise?

Again, we can only speculate on the actions of those written about in the *Sagas*, but what we can do is consider what elements were important to the ability to communicate and prophesise or to work seidr sorcery. In deconstructing the examples, we can look to put together our own rites with a renewed understanding of what might have contributed to making them possible. Therefore, if we decide that the energy of the hearts was the important element, we can look to raising energy as being an important part of our rites. If we decide that the understanding of the animals is important, we can seek to build a strong familiarity and connection to the land that

---

[489] Jones, *Erik the Red and Other Icelandic Sagas.* 1961.
[490] Wallis, *Shamans/Neo-Shamans.* 2003.
[491] Ibid.

we are looking to prophesise within through utiseta and communicating with the land. If it is animal or bird language that we wish to learn, we can study and honour individual animals in order to work with their spirit forms.

My understanding is that the energy which comes from dancing, drumming, and the Vardlokkurs helps to initiate the altered state of the seidkona, as well as creating a battery and food for those beings who do not have a physical existence. It allows them to act on the physical plane and to therefore interact with us. Of course, this is a personal theory, and as such is subject to deep scrutiny. Your personal theories might be different or they might be similar but built on further research and ideas. Either way, build and work within the constructs of your own spiritual beliefs and understanding.

THE SHAKING TRANCE

In Seidways, Jan Fries acquaints seidr with a particular kind of trance work – that of the shaking trance. He describes a specific way of inducing a shaking as part of ecstatic trance which involves a slow build up of energy. Fries also demonstrated examples of ecstatic communities, both contemporary and in antiquity; who had elements of shaking within their religious rites. Although he clearly states that:

> "As far as I know, there exists no full proof that the seidmages of the old north actually shook while they tranced, prophesised, or projected glamours."[492]

Many people took the shaking trance as being strongly associated with the act of seidr. This leaves us with the question of whether you need to shake to seidr, and what happens if you don't shake? Fries introduced us to a rich pedigree of shakers, from the Pythia of Delphi in the Classical World, through to the Christian Shakers and the Welsh Awenyddion.[493] Kaldera and Filan give us this example of the Huguenots in the Cevannes Mountains:

> "Prophets and prophetesses would fall to the ground violently; contemporary witnesses described them as 'shaking their heads, crawling on the floor, quaking and trembling, drumming, trumpeting, thundering,

---

[492] Fries, *Seidways*. 1996.
[493] Ibid.

snuffling, blowing as with a horn, panting, sighing, groaning, hissing, laughing, pointing, shaking, threshing, using childish repetition, howling like a dog, and generally acting in a disorderly fashion.[494]

Lindquist, writing about Yggdrasil, also showed how the seidr trance could involve shaking:

"Entranced, Peter clutches his staff spasmodically, his body wriggling and twisting in what looks like epileptic convulsions"[495]

Shaking was found where possession and trance took place. For both the Shakers and the Huguenots, this possession took the form of the Holy Spirit which entered a person whilst they were in an altered state. For the Shakers, this Holy Spirit caused them to shake, and writhe, and speak in tongues as they channelled *"the living energy of Christ by becoming its vessel."*[496] For the Huguenots, their shaking and writhing stopped once the Holy Spirit entered them, from which point they would *"stop their convulsions and speak in a clear, calm manner."*[497] We see the Christian Shaking tradition continuing with contemporary churches such as the Pentecostals.

Fries tells us that within shamanic communities, sometimes a child would begin to shake during shamanic rites and that this shaking showed that they would be likely to later become a shaman themselves.

As we can see, shaking has a firm pedigree and is found in many different possession and trance rites. But what role does the shaking have? And what happens if during a rite you don't shake? Fries' shaking practice fascinated and interested me and as such we experimented greatly with the shaking, specifically inducing it in ritual, and evaluating what role it played when it happened spontaneously in rites. From my understanding, it seems that it is likely that the shaking is a side effect of the build up of energy. Sometimes the shaking seemed to magnify the trance state, but there didn't seem to be a lack of trance of effectiveness in the seidr work when there was no shaking. The amount of people present at a rite also did not make a difference to the shaking. The one thing that seemed to be a factor was that when a greater amount of energy was raised

---

494 Filan & Kaldera, *Drawing Down the Spirits*. 2009.
495 Lindquist, *Shamanic Performances on the Urban Scene*. 1997.
496 Fries, *Seidways*. 1996.
497 Filan & Kaldera, *Drawing Down the Spirits*. 2009.

at the beginning of a rite, but fewer questions were asked, or less active sorcery was done, there was more shaking. Therefore, it seems likely that the shaking itself is induced by an excess of energy, energy that isn't being used specifically in the rite itself.

Shaking induced by an excess of energy can also be seen naturally within the body. Anger, fear, excitement, and grief can all induce shaking through a build up of energy and release of hormones. Often, the subdued and controlled emotional outbursts (without the shouting and throwing things!) are the ones that induce the most shaking, as the extra energy seeks to free itself. Another point where the body could be seen as freeing itself from excess energy is in the cold where the movement of shaking also helps the body to keep warm. Sexual energy, in the build up to and release of orgasm can also manifest in shaking.

Is the shaking, therefore, a sign of excess energy? This is understandable when energy has been raised through ecstatic dancing and drumming. It is also understandable within possession, where a foreign energy is thought to enter the body in order to communicate and partly take control for awhile. After both possession[498] and trance work, the shaman can also display energy release symptoms such as tears or laughter.

IS SEIDR SHAMANISM?

Contemporary seidr is very often described as a kind of shamanism, or sometimes even more specifically as 'Norse Shamanism'.[499] Can we, and should we, describe seidr as shamanism? If shamanism is not the right terminology, is there a better one? Blain uses the term shamanistic;[500] is this better, and if so, what makes it more acceptable?

The term Shaman was used originally to describe accounts of the Tungus and Evenki speaking people's ecstatic practices in Siberia.[501] It was used within this very specific ethnographic and anthropological setting but, once used, fast became used by anthropologists and ethnographers to describe the practices that they found

---

[498] Filan & Kaldera, *Drawing Down the Spirits*. 2009.
[499] Chisholm & Flowers (eds), *A Source-book of Seid*. 2002.
[500] Wallis, *Shamans/Neo-Shamans*. 2003.
[501] Blain, *Nine Worlds of Seid-Magic*. 2001.

within other cultures that held similar ideas and activities.[502] This soon meant that the term Shaman began to represent a whole range of ecstatic and trance techniques. This was particularly so in 1960s America where the word shaman was soon used to describe *"any tribal practitioner of magic."*[503] Ronald Hutton points out that this trend was found a lot less within British anthropologists who had a range of terms they used which meant that they could describe techniques individually rather than rely on *'shaman'* as a catch all. This leaves us with the question of what actually determines shamanism. Do we look to only those practices from Siberia that originally birthed the term? Or do we look on a grander scale and follow and examine the practices from around the world that were described as shamanic? The problem is magnified when we remember that, like seidr, shamanism was not simply one set of people with one set of practices. Rather, Siberian shamanism covers a wide area with different tribes and different people all who might have slightly different ideas and practices.[504]

To confound the confusion, not surprisingly, the term was then picked up by the Western Occult and New Age movement, this spread helped by the spread of Michael Harner's book *The Way of the Shaman*. Since then, the term shaman has become synonymous with trance and altered states, astral and inner journeying, and communication with *'other'* based on these techniques. The induction of altered states using drumming and dancing also plays a large part in shamanic activities.

Michael Harner was a Professor of Anthropology who, once experiencing various indigenous shamanic cultural practices was inspired to investigate trance and journeying techniques and created a western shamanism.[505] Harner's *'core shamanism'*[506] took shamanic motifs that were found in multiple indigenous cultures and put them together to create a shamanic program that stood outside of any particular culture but that equally could then be applied universally. These motifs included initiation, journeying to the underworld and upper world, spiritual healing, and

---

[502] Wallis, *Shamans/Neo-Shamans*. 2003.
[503] Hutton, *The Shamans of Siberia*. 1993.
[504] Ibid.
[505] Wallis, *Shamans/Neo-Shamans*. 2003.
[506] Harner, *The Way of the Shaman*. 1992.

working with spirit and animal helpers. His trance triggers were considered to be *'safer'* than many of the traditional trance triggers in that he relied on drumming rather than on hallucinogens.

Harner's shamanism was accessible to all. Whereas in tribal cultures the shaman was someone whose whole life and calling was devoted to their craft, Harner's students became *'weekend shamans'*. Instead of the shaman being unique and being one of a select few, anyone could become a shaman; they just needed the right book or the right workshop. A shaman in tribal society didn't always set out to be a shaman, instead the spirits chose them.[507] The shaman was rarely impressed with this turn of events but was not able to refuse the calling. Harner's shamans choose their shamanism and go looking for the spirits. Another difference is that Harner shamans' questioners (those that they are working for) take the journey themselves, or accompany the shaman on the journey. In tribal societies this would have been considered far too dangerous. A journey was taken by the shaman, on behalf of the questioner because they had both the ability to do it and the protection from the spirits themselves.[508]

Shamanism then becomes something that involves an altered state of consciousness (or trance state), described by Harner as SSC, a shamanic state of consciousness.[509] Harner's definition of a shaman is:

> *"a man or woman who enters an altered state of consciousness – at will – to contact and utilise an ordinarily hidden reality in order to acquire knowledge, power, and to help other persons. The shaman has at least one, and usually more, "spirits" in his personal service."*[510]

Does this sound similar to seidr? Certainly, we have found examples of seidr that show someone willingly entering an altered state, with that state being used to acquire knowledge and sometimes being used to acquire and direct power. The *Greenland Saga*[511] shows us that Thorbjorg was able to commune with spirits, but did she have them in her personal service, or was she simply

---

[507] Hutton, *The Shamans of Siberia*. 1993.

[508] Wallis, *Shamans/Neo-Shamans*. 2003.

[509] Ibid.

[510] Harner, *The Way of the Shaman*. 1992.

[511] Jones, *Erik the Red and Other Icelandic Sagas*. 1961.

talking to the spirits that resided in the land she was visiting? We could also consider the fylgia and the hugr as being spirits that the seidr workers had in their personal service, but didn't everyone have these? Therefore, what separates the shaman from the ordinary person? Yet, is there a difference? Although the Siberians believed that it took a special calling and specialist skills to become a shaman, Harner's book allows anyone to pick up the mantle and the title. Can we take Harner's description of shamanism and put it onto seidr? Possibly, although Hutton points out that Harner's definition of shamanism would also include cunning folk.[512] Were the British cunning folk not that dissimilar to shamans, however, living outside of the village community and taking an active spiritual role?

Mircea Eliade, in his book *Shamanism*, on the other hand, describes shamanism as soul travel to an upper world.[513] Contemporary seidr high seat rites more often involve travel to a lower world rather than to an upper world.

In chapter eight we looked at the similarities between seidr and the shamanistic practices of their neighbours. The Siberian shamans in particular had certain elements to their shamanism. The first was that the world was divided into three levels with many tribes seeing the world as a tree.[514] The Norse had Yggdrasil as the tree of life. There was also a belief in the world of spirit, with these spirits often being animals.[515] The Siberians controlled their spirits with human specialists (shamans),[516] and the Norse concept of hugr showed that a part of the soul of a skilled person could be harnessed for seidr and sorcery. The Shamans were separate to religion; the Siberians had priests who dealt with religion but the shaman served their communities in a separate way.[517] The Norse had (gothi) who dealt with matters of religion, the Volva and Seidr workers were separate to this. In Chukchee shamanism, the shaman *'sinks'* as he visits other worlds,[518] similarly,

---

512 Hutton, *The Shamans of Siberia*. 2007.
513 Eliade, *Shamanism*. 1989.
514 Hutton, *The Shamans of Siberia*. 2007.
515 Ibid.
516 Ibid.
517 Ibid.
518 Ibid.

Voluspa describes the Volva sinking as she finishes prophesising.

Interestingly, many of these examples can also be transposed to other cultures and religious practices. This is what makes it so easy to borrow the term shaman in describing a whole range of ecstatic techniques. It is why Harner describes shamanism as being a basic component of human society[519] - the idea of an altered state of consciousness, astral travel, and contact with the spirit world is prevalent in so many different indigenous (and also contemporary) cultures. Should it all be described as shamanism?

Jenny Blain (on asking whether seidr is shamanism) asks whether we have a suitable enough definition for shamanism to be able to do so at all.[520] I concur and query whether we realistically even have a suitable enough definition of seidr in order to ask the question. If seidr covers many different practices and is difficult to pin down a definition for, and shamanism gives us the same problems, then how can we possibly seek to understand whether seidr is the same as shamanism and whether it can be described using the term shamanic? Blain also gives us another problem, in that the term *'shaman'* was honorary and therefore it can be suggested that you can't call yourself a shaman, someone else needs to do that.[521]

Will we ever, therefore, be able to give seidr the title of shamanism? The questions surrounding this are so wide and varied that I believe that Blain's use of the term shamanistic is far more suitable. Yet, were all elements of seidr in the *Sagas* and *Eddas* shamanistic? Again, we are left with the problem that seidr covers so many areas that it is impossible to look back at antiquity and show every example to be shamanistic. The same goes for contemporary seidr, whilst one group or one person's practice might be shamanistic, another's may not be. On the whole, however, I believe that it is helpful to use the term shamanistic when describing seidr practice both in antiquarian and contemporary usage.

---

[519] Harner, *The Way of the Shaman.* 1992.
[520] Blain, *Nine Worlds of Seid-Magic.* 2001.
[521] Ibid.

IS THE HIGH SEAT MEDIUMSHIP?

Within the Victorian era, a renewed interest in ghost stories and the supernatural gave rise to the new tradition of Spiritualism.[522] Spiritualists were those who believed in life after death and sought contact with those who had died through communication with their spirits. A spiritualist medium was someone who could speak to the dead, and as spiritualism matured, could also channel and allow the dead to speak through them, as well as being able to manifest them through ectoplasm. The spiritualist medium became a dinner party favourite, travelling around homes and contacting spirits,[523] allowing us to draw parallels with the Norse Volvas who travelled from farmstead to farmstead, prophesising during winter feasts.[524] The majority of the spiritualist mediums at the beginning of spiritualism were women, and this became one of the few occupations that allowed women to make a comfortable and independent living.[525]

As discussed in chapter eight, although many Victorians believed in spiritualism, there were just as many who were incredibly sceptical, and with new breakthroughs in technology such as glowing paint and photography, the ability to fake[526] spiritual contact was available in abundance. Unfortunately, the trickery and fraud has overshadowed much of the spiritualist movement during those times and as such, it is difficult to judge how much of the spiritual contact happened without additional 'help'.

Over the last thirty years spiritualists and mediums and those who claim to be able to speak with and pass on messages from the dead to the living (and vice versa) have become widespread. Many of these have written and published books and have appeared on television.[527] For every famous spiritualist, there are many who are unknown, or who have built up local fame and reputation performing in church and village halls. They provide a service for those who have lost loved ones and are looking

---

522 Pearsall, *Table-rappers*. 2004.
523 Ibid.
524 Chisholm & Flowers (eds), *A Source-book of Seid*. 2002.
525 Pearsall, *Table-rappers*. 2004.
526 Ibid.
527 For example David Wells, Doris Stokes, Derek Acorah.

for comfort.[528] There are many spiritualist churches and groups across the UK providing that gateway between the living and the dead. Like the High Seat, or seidhjallr, contemporary spiritualists also use a raised platform (often the stage at the front of a church or village hall) to separate them from their audience.

Looking at the way that our high seat rite is conducted, and looking at the description of Thorbjorg's prophesising within the *Greenland Saga*[529] it is not a huge leap to suggest that seidr prophecy is very similar to spiritualist mediumship. In many ways, the examples of prophecy within the *Sagas* has more in common with this tradition than it does with, for example, something like shamanism. Lindquist suggests that:

> *"mediums do not journey and their interaction with spirits takes the form of possession; they allow spirits to enter their bodies, making them a vehicle for the spirit, while a shaman interacts with spirits, so to speak, on an equal footing."*[530]

Within seidr, does the communication with spirits come from possession or from journeying and interaction? Is there a difference in this answer when it comes to seidr in antiquity as opposed to contemporary seidr?

Within contemporary seidr, not all seidr workers use journeying and don't use possession; Blain describes instances of the gods' possessing Seers whilst on the high seat.[531] It can also be said that not all mediums use possession in order to receive messages. Doris Stokes[532] explains that the spirits talk to her as voices that she hears in her head (or in her ear) and that they explain to her the messages she needs to pass on.

There is a theory that when working with spirits and asking for them to interact (through Ouija boards or manifestation in some other way) one person acts as the medium and one person works as the channel.[533] The medium's role is to provide the energy for the spirit to use to manifest, and the channel's role is to provide the body for the spirit to use to manifest. Interestingly, it seems that

---

[528] Acorah and Sutton, *The Psychic World of Derek Acorah*. 1999.
[529] Jones, *Erik the Red and Other Icelandic Sagas*. 1961.
[530] Lindquist, *Shamanic Performances on the Urban Scene*. 1997.
[531] Blain, *Nine Worlds of Seid-Magic*. 2001.
[532] Stokes and Dearsley, *More Voices in My Ear*. 1980.
[533] Fiosa, *A Voice in the Forest*. 2004.

some people are better at acting as the medium and some are better at acting as the channel.[534] Is this concept found within the seidr high seat rite?

In looking at the high seat rite in relation to spiritualist mediumship we can see a number of similarities, but in the same way as seidr and shamanism refer to a range of differing practices, we can also see that spiritualist and platform mediums also have a number of differences within their techniques. Certainly, Thorbjorg in the *Greenland Saga* works in an exceptionally similar way to a spiritualist medium, but is this enough to generalise?

---

[534] Fiosa, *A Voice in the Forest.* 2004.

CONCLUSION

The Gate is Open is the product of more than a decade of researching, experimenting, and evaluating. It seems, however, still to be only a scratch on the surface of my work with seidr, with hopefully a lifetime more researching, experimenting, and evaluating to come. The term seidr has been used within antiquity for many different practices, and those we have covered in this book range from prophecy and divination, through to sorcery and witchcraft. In contemporary use, seidr has grown and grown, encompassing a wealth of practices, ideas, and people. Although the rediscovery of seidr has been happening since at least the 1990s (and almost certainly before that), it feels to me as though many more people are becoming acquainted with the practices, and that we are sitting on the tip of an iceberg that will encompass much more activity before too long. And yet, the roots of seidr are so very human, so very practical, that it is almost as though they didn't really need to be rediscovered and that humanity always knew how to reach them, and work with them.

The practical elements in this book have been the product of experiment and practice. If something worked, we kept it, if it didn't, we tried again. Every rite I am a part of, every talk I give, new ideas are born, and these almost always come from people asking questions. Why do you do that in that way? What would happen if you did this instead? Have you thought about trying it this way? The rites exist in the form that they do at the time of print, but the reality is that they will continue to be adapted and changed. Therefore, please make sure that you do the same. Work out what works for you and for your group and don't be afraid to make changes. Use this book as examples and inspiration and put together practices that fit you and the groups you are part of. Read as many people's ideas and research on seidr as you can, and if you get the chance to, practice with as many people as you feel comfortable working magically with. At present there are still not enough practical books available on seidr, but I hope that slowly that will change. Where the raw sources are not available in antiquity, look for areas that you can borrow from; after all, there is evidence to suggest that our Norse forebears did the same.

Over the last ten years infinitely more sources have become available on the subject of seidr, and hopefully - over the next ten years and onwards - that number will double, and triple. I hope that you will feel inspired to build your own practices and share them with other practitioners through future blogs and books. One thing is certain: the seidr current is fresh and vibrant, with the strength and solidity of the Norse deities behind it.

FURTHER READING

Although it could be said that less information exists on seidr and northern tradition witchcraft than on many of the other neo-pagan and reconstructed pagan practices, there is more information *'out there'* than you see at first glance.

Many of the texts I have quoted and listed below are out of print, and some had small print runs as *'limited interest'* books. Over the last ten years of my research, more and more avenues have become available for reading this kind of text. Whereas in the early days of researching I spent many years sitting in the reading room at the British Library, over the last few years electronic copies of out of print books, online article libraries, and basic reprints of the more popular out of print books have kept me working steadily at home in the warm.

I absolutely recommend trawling through the older texts.

RECOMMENDED READING

PRIMARY SOURCES

The Prose Edda
The Younger Edda, Snorri Sturluson
Erik the Red and the Greenland Sagas
The Saga of the Volsungs
Egil's Saga
Heimskringla
Njal's Saga
The Danish History of Saxo Grammaticus
Orkneyinga Saga
The Germania, Tacitus
Laxdaela Saga

SECONDARY SOURCES

Adalsteinsson, Jon Hnefill. *Under the Cloak*

Blain, Jenny. *Nine Worlds of Seid-Magic.*

Blain, Jenny Marion Margaret. *Wights and Ancestors: Heathenism in a Living Landscape.*

Chisholm, James; Flowers, Stephen. *A Source-book of Seid*

Crossley-Holland, Kevin. *The Penguin Book of Norse Myths: Gods of the Vikings*

Dronke, Ursula. *Myth and Fiction in Early Norse Lands.*

Dubois, Thomas A. *Nordic Religions in the Viking Age.*

Edred, Thorsson. *Witchdom of the True*

Ellis, H R. *The Road to Hel - A Study of the Conception of the Dead in Old Norse Literature.*

Filan, Kenaz, and Raven Kaldera. *Drawing Down the Spirits*

Fries, Jan. *Seidways: Shaking, Swaying and Serpent Mysteries*

Jochens, Jenny. *Old Norse Images of Women.*

Lindquist, Galina. *Shamanic Performances on the Urban Scene*

McGrath, Sheena. *Asyniur: Women's Mysteries in the Northern Tradition*

Morris, Katherine. *Sorceress or Witch*

Nasstrom, Britt-Mari. *Freyja: The Great Goddess of the North*

O'Donoghue, Heather. *From Asgard to Valhalla: The Remarkable History of the Norse Myths*

Paxson, Diana, *Essential Asatru*

Paxson, Diana L. "The Return of the Volva." *Mountain Thunder*, Summer 1993.

———. *Trance-Portation: Learning to Navigate the Inner World*

Strömbäck, Dag, Bo Almqvist, Gidlund Gidlund, and Hans Mebius. *Sejd*

Wallis, Robert J. *Shamans/Neo-Shamans*

COMPARATIVE

Cambrensis, Gerald of Wales *The Journey Through Wales and the Description of Wales.*

Davies, Owen. *Cunning-folk: Popular Magic in English History*

D'Este, Sorita (editor) *Priestesses Pythonesses Sibyls*

Eliade, Mircea. *Shamanism: Archaic Techniques of Ecstasy*

Harner, Michael. *The Way of the Shaman*

Hutton, Ronald. *Shamans: Siberian Spirituality and the Western Imagination*

Homer, *The Odyssey*

Elias Lonrot, *The Kalevala*

Ogden, Daniel. *Greek and Roman Necromancy*

BIBLIOGRAPHY

Acorah, Derek, and John Sutton. *The Psychic World of Derek Acorah: Discover How to Develop Your Hidden Powers.* Piatkus Books, 1999.

Adalsteinsson, Jon Hnefill. *Under the Cloak: The Acceptance of Christianity in Iceland with Particular Reference to the Religious Attitudes Prevailing at the Time.* Haskolautgafan, 1979.

Aswynn, Freya. *Leaves of Yggdrasil: A Synthesis of Rune Gods' Magic Feminine Mysteries Folklore.* 1st ed. Aswynn (London), 1988.

Blain, Jenny. *Nine Worlds of Seid-Magic.* Routledge, 2001.

———. *Wights and Ancestors: Heathenism in a Living Landscape.* In *Wyrd's Well,* 2000.

Bonser, W. *The Magic of the Finns.* In *Folklore* Vol. 35, 1924.

Byock, Jesse L. *The Saga of the Volsungs: The Norse Epic of Sigurd the Dragon Slayer.* Penguin Classics, 2004.

Cambrensis, Gerald of Wales Giraldus. *The Journey Through Wales and the Description of Wales.* Penguin Classics, 2004.

Carr-Gomm, Philip. *The Druid Way.* Illustrated edition. Thorsons, 1993.

Chisholm, James; Flowers, Stephen. *A Source-book of Seid,* Runa Raven Press, 2002

Colum, Padraic. *The King of Ireland's Son: An Irish Folk Tale.* 8th ed. Floris Books, 1986.

Craigie, W. A. *The Oldest Icelandic Folklore.* In *Folklore* Vol. 4, 1893.

Crooke, William. *Introduction to the Popular Religion and Folklore of Northern India.* 1894th ed. Asian Educational Services, India, 2007.

Crossley-Holland, Kevin. *The Penguin Book of Norse Myths: Gods of the Vikings.* New Ed. Penguin, 1996.

Cunningham, Scott. *Magical Aromatherapy: The Power of Scent.* Llewellyn Publications, U.S., 1989.

Dante. *Dante: Inferno.* Penguin Classics, 2006.

Dasent, George Webbe. *Popular Tales From the Norse.* Forgotten Books, 2008.

Davidson, Hilda Ellis. *Journey to the Other World: Papers from the Exeter Conference, 1971.* DS Brewer, 1975.

Davies, Owen. *Cunning-folk: Popular Magic in English History.* Illustrated edition. Hambledon Continuum, 2003.

———. *Popular Magic: Cunning-folk in English History.* New Ed. Hambledon Continuum, 2007.

d'Este, Sorita. *Towards the Wiccan Circle - A Practical Introduction to the Principles of Wicca.* Avalonia, 2008.

Dickens, Charles. *The Christmas Books: A Christmas Carol, the Chimes, the Cricket On the Hearth.* New Ed. Penguin Classics, 2007.

Dronke, Ursula. *Myth and Fiction in Early Norse Lands.* Variorum, 1996.

Dubois, Thomas A. *Nordic Religions in the Viking Age.* University of Pennsylvania Press, 1999.

Eiriksson, Leifur. *Egil's Saga.* Penguin Classics, 2004.

Eliade, Mircea. *Shamanism: Archaic Techniques of Ecstasy.* New edition. Arkana, 1989.

Ellis, H R. *The Road to Hel - A Study of the Conception of the Dead in Old Norse Literature.* Cambridge University Press, 1943.

Farrar, Janet, Caroline Tully, Kim Huggens, Naomi Ozaniec, Vivienne O'Regan, and Sorita D'Este. *Priestesses Pythonesses Sibyls: An Anthology of Essays Regarding Trance, Possession and Mantic States. Women Who Speak with and for the Gods.* Avalonia, 2008.

Farrar, Stewart. *What Witches Do: A Modern Coven Revealed.* New edition. Phoenix Publishing Inc., U.S., 1989.

Faulkes, Anthony. *Edda.* New Ed. Phoenix, 1995.

Filan, Kenaz, and Raven Kaldera. *Drawing Down the Spirits: The Traditions and Techniques of Spirit Possession.* Inner Traditions / Destiny Books, 2009.

Fiosa, Jimahl Di. *A Voice in the Forest: Spirit Conversations with Alex Sanders.* Harvest Shadows Publications, 2004.

Fries, Jan. *Seidways: Shaking, Swaying and Serpent Mysteries.* Ill. Mandrake of Oxford, 1996.

———. *Visual Magick: A Manual of Freestyle Shamanism.* 2nd ed. Mandrake of Oxford, 2000.

Galt, John. *The Spaewife: A Tale of the Scottish Chronicles,* Volume I: 1. Bastian Books, 2008.

Gerrard, Katie. *Odin's Gateways: A Practical Guide to the Wisdom of the Runes, Through Galdr, Sigils and Casting.* Avalonia, 2009.

Gittings, Clare. *Death, Burial and the Individual in Early Modern England.* Routledge, 1984.

Grammaticus, Saxo. *The Danish History of Saxo Grammaticus.* Forgotten Books, 2008.

Gundarsson, Kveldulf. *Teutonic Religion: Folk Beliefs and Practices of the Northern Tradition.* Llewellyn Publications, U.S., 1993.

Gylfason, Thorsteinn. *Njal's Saga.* New edition. Wordsworth Editions Ltd, 1998.

Harner, Michael. *The Way of the Shaman.* Third edition. Harper, San Francisco, 1992.

Harris-Logan, Stuart A. *Singing with Blackbirds: The Survival of Primal Celtic Shamanism in Later Folk-Traditions.* Grey House in the Woods, 2006.

Homer. *The Odyssey.* Rev Ed. Penguin Classics, 2003.

Hutton, Ronald. *Shamans: Siberian Spirituality and the Western Imagination.* New Ed. Hambledon Continuum, 2007.

———. *Shamans: Siberian Spirituality and Western Imagination.* Illustrated edition. Hambledon Continuum, 2001.

———. *The Shamans of Siberia.* The Isle of Avalon Press, Somerset, 1993.

Jochens, Jenny. *Old Norse Images of Women.* University of Pennsylvania Press, 1996.

———. *Women in Old Norse Society.* Reprint. Cornell University Press, 1998.

John, Runic. *The Book of Seidr: The Native English and Northern European Shamanic Tradition.* Capall Bann Publishing, 2004.

Jones, Gwyn. *Erik the Red and Other Icelandic Sagas.* Reprint. Oxford University Press, 1961.

Jordan, Michael. *Witches: An Encyclopedia of Paganism and Magic.* Kyle Cathie, 1996.

Kerényi, C. *The Heroes of the Greeks.* Thames & Hudson, 1978.

Larrington, Carolyne. *The Poetic Edda.* Oxford Paperbacks, 1999.

Leach, Maria. *Funk and Wagnall's Standard Dictionary of Folklore, Mythology and Legend.* New English Library Ltd, 1975.

Lindquist, Galina. *Shamanic Performances on the Urban Scene: Neo-shamanism in Contemporary Sweden.* Stockholm Studies in Social Anthropology, 1997.

Lönnrot, Elias. *The Kalevala.* New edition. Oxford Paperbacks, 1999.

Mackenzie, Alexander. *The Prophecies of the Brahan Seer.* Constable, 1983.

Magnusson, Magnus, Mark Harrison, Keith Durham, and Ian Heath. *The Vikings: Voyagers of Discovery and Plunder.* Osprey Publishing, 2008.

Magnusson, Magnus, and Hermann Palsson. *Laxdaela Saga.* Reissue. Penguin Classics, 1975.

McGrath, Sheena. *Asyniur: Women's Mysteries in the Northern Tradition.* Capall Bann Publishing, 1997.

Morris, Katherine. *Sorceress or Witch: Image of Gender in Mediaeval Iceland and Northern Europe.* University Press of America, 1991.

Nasstrom, Britt-Mari. *Freyja: The Great Goddess of the North.* Almqvist & Wiksell Internat., 1995.

None. *Orkneyinga Saga: The History of the Earls of Orkney.* New Ed. Penguin Classics, 2004.

O'Donoghue, Heather. *From Asgard to Valhalla: The Remarkable History of the Norse Myths*. I B Tauris & Co Ltd, 2008.

Ogden, Daniel. *Greek and Roman Necromancy*. New edition. Princeton University Press, 2004.

Palsson, Hermann. *Voluspa: The Sybil's Prophecy*. Lockharton P., 1996.

Palsson, Hermann, and Paul Edwards. *Gautrek's Saga*. Hodder & Stoughton Ltd, 1968.

Paxson, Diana L. "*The Return of the Volva.*" In *Mountain Thunder*, Summer 1993.

———. *Trance-Portation: Learning to Navigate the Inner World*. Red Wheel/Weiser, 2008.

———. *Essential Asatru, Norse Paganism*. New Age, n.d.

Pearsall, Ronald. *Table-rappers: The Victorians and the Occult*. New Ed. The History Press Ltd, 2004.

Pennick, Nigel. *Practical Magic in the Northern Tradition*. 2nd ed. Thoth Publications, 1994.

———. *Secrets of East Anglian Magic*. 2nd ed. Capall Bann Publishing, 2004.

Ready, Romilla, and Kate Burton. *Neuro-linguistic Programming (NLP) Workbook for Dummies*. John Wiley & Sons, 2008.

Roth, Gabrielle. *Ecstatic Dance*. Sounds True Inc, 2004.

Shandler, Nina. *The Strange Case of Hellish Nell: The True Story of Helen Duncan and the Witch Trial of World War II*. Da Capo Press Inc, 2006.

Simpson, Jacqueline. *Be Bold, but not too Bold*, In *Folklore* Vol 102, 1991.

Stokes, Doris, and Linda Dearsley. *More Voices in My Ear*. Futura Publications, 1980.

Strömbäck, Dag, Bo Almqvist, Gidlund Gidlund, and Hans Mebius. *Sejd: och andra studier i nordisk själsuppfattning*. Kungl. Gustav Adolfs Akademien för svensk folkkultur, Gidlunds förlag, 2000.

Sturlason, Snorre. *Heimskringla or the Lives of the Norse Kings*. Kessinger Publishing Co, 2004.

Sturluson, Snorri Webbe. *Heimskringla: The Chronicle of the Kings of Norway*. Forgotten Books, 2008.

Sutherland, Elizabeth. *The Seer of Kintail*. New Ed. Constable, 1996.

Tacitus. *Agricola and Germania*. Penguin Classics, 2010.

Thorsson, Edred. *Witchdom of the True*. Runa Raven Press, 1999.

Titchenell, Elsa-Brita. *The Masks of Odin: Wisdom of the Ancient Norse*. Theosophical University Press, 1968.

Virgil. *The Aeneid*. Rev Ed. Penguin Classics, 2003.

Wallis, Robert J. *Shamans/Neo-Shamans: Ecstasies, Alternative Archaeologies and Contemporary Pagans*. 1st edn. Routledge, 2003.

INDEX

A

Aesir 34, 37, 47, 86, 148, 150, 151, 152, 153
Amber 87
Ancestors 35, 37, 47, 48, 77, 82, 90, 99, 100, 119, 121, 123, 124, 126, 127, 128, 132, 136, 138, 141, 160, 161, 164, 182
Arrow-Odd's Saga 15, 53, 54, 69, 111
Asgard ...20, 32, 33, 47, 104, 124, 129, 148, 160, 161, 172

B

Baldr 40, 41, 42, 44, 145, 153
Baldr's Dreams 40, 42, 44
Blot 141
Book of Llandaff 129
Brunhild 42, 81

C

Cloak .48, 50, 51, 59, 84, 87, 100, 101, 102, 103, 105, 120, 121, 159, 160
Codex Regis 14, 33

D

Dionysus 36
Diplomatarium Islandicum 67
Disir ...23, 38, 40, 45, 47, 48, 59, 73, 85, 86, 88, 97, 122, 135, 136, 137, 138, 139, 140, 141, 142, 143, 146

E

Egil's Saga .. 13, 15, 106, 129
Elder Edda ...... 14, *See* Poetic Edda
Ergi 162, 164, 165, 166, 167, 168, 171
Erik the Red ... 13, 15, 50, 51, 83, 95, 100, 103, 110, 127, 173, 183, 188, 192
Eyrbyggja Saga 67

F

Fenris 152
Finnish .. 61, 69, 81, 98, 101, 108, 109, 110, 112, 172, 173, 176
Fraekna 33
Freyja 31, 34, 36, 37, 38, 52, 83, 86, 88, 102, 106, 119, 121, 124, 137, 148, 150, 151, 157, 158, 159
Freyr 148, 149, 169
Fridhjolf's Saga 33, 70, 71, 95
Frigga 37, 40, 102, 137, 144, 145, 148, 152, 153, 174
Fylgia 70, 73, 124, 125, 164, 189

G

Garm 42, 106
Gautrek's Saga 149
Gisli Saga 98
Gongu-Hrolf's Saga 65, 66, 112

Greenland Saga 15, 50, 51, 57, 66, 80, 81, 83, 95, 106, 110, 112, 127, 173, 182, 188, 192, 193
Grettirs Saga 129
Grimnir 36, 174
Gullveig 34, 36, 37
Gylfaginning 42
Gythia 154

H

Harald War-Tooth's Saga .. 69
Harbard's Song 103, 105
Havardr Saga 125
Heid ... 32, 33, 34, 35, 36, 44, 45, 53, 59, 60
Heimdall 160, 161
Heimskingla 165
Hel 37, 40, 42, 43, 47, 48, 81, 86, 88, 103, 105, 106, 107, 108, 119, 121, 129, 152, 174
Helheim .. 37, 40, 42, 43, 44, 46, 47, 48, 64, 81, 86, 87, 88, 89, 90, 91, 92, 93, 97, 103, 105, 106, 107, 108, 113, 117, 118, 119, 120, 121, 124, 152, 160, 180, 182
Hermodr 42, 44
High Seat 13, 24, 25, 41, 43, 48, 50, 52, 54, 59, 61, 64, 79, 80, 83, 84, 85, 87, 89, 90, 92, 94, 95, 96, 97, 98, 100, 101, 103, 105, 107, 109, 110, 111, 112, 113, 114, 115, 116, 117, 118, 119, 121, 129, 141, 146, 160, 161, 165, 180, 189, 191, 192, 193
Hrafnar ... 43, 64, 77, 79, 80, 81, 82, 83, 98, 100, 107, 149, 153
Hrolf Kraki's Saga 15, 33, 53, 71
Hugr .. 66, 67, 68, 69, 70, 71, 72, 73, 75, 124, 125, 164, 189

I

Incense 21, 22, 38, 39, 40, 45, 47, 81, 84, 85, 116, 119, 138, 139, 146, 158, 160

J

Jormungard 152

K

Kalevala 108, 175

L

Landnamabok 15, 33, 53
Laxdaela Saga 13, 15, 53, 56, 65, 98, 128, 129, 130, 163, 165, 168, 197
Lokasenna ... 101, 106, 109, 151, 165, 166, 167
Loki ... 36, 40, 41, 102, 151, 152, 166

M

Mimir 35, 36, 151
Muspelheim 105

N

Niflheim 40, 43, 106
Night Mare 67, 68
Njal's Saga ... 53, 65, 69, 137
Njord 148
Nornagestr 55
Norns ... 82, 136, 137, 143, 144, 145, 146, 147, 152

O

Odin 20, 23, 32, 33, 34, 35, 36, 37, 40, 41, 42, 43, 44, 45, 46, 47, 48, 53, 73, 81, 83, 85, 86, 88, 101, 103, 106, 109, 119, 121, 129, 134, 144, 148, 149, 151,

152, 154, 160, 161, 166, 174, 177
Odin's Gateways. 20, 23, 73, 85
Olaf's Saga...................... 14
Orkneyingasaga 55, 163, 171
Orlog............. 143, 145, 146
Orpheus................. 107, 108

P

Persephone 108
Poetic Edda ... 14, 32, 35, 40, 41, 42, 86, 101, 103, 106, 107, 109, 128, 137, 143, 150, 151, 153, 166, 174, 175
Prose Edda............... 14, 197

R

Ragnorak 32, 145

S

Saga of Hakon the Good ... 71
Saga of Olaf Tryggvason ... 71
Sami ... 61, 69, 81, 98, 101, 104, 109, 112, 162, 170, 172, 173, 174, 176
Saxo Grammaticus..... 43, 58, 111, 149, 168, 169
Seidhjallr 13, 14, 63, 64, 65, 66, 70, 71, 79, 80, 98, 99, 100, 103, 104, 173, 174, 176, 192, *See* High Seat
Seidkona 15, 31, 33, 50, 65, 67, 69, 70, 71, 98, 99, 100, 154, 184
Sessrumnir 124, 150
Skuld..................... 144, 147
Sleipnir .. 40, 43, 44, 47, 48, 154, 166
Spae 54, 55, 56, 57
Spakona..................... 54, 57
Sturlungasaga................. 125
Sturluson, Snorri 14

T

Taliesin............................ 36
The Brahan Seer 56
The King of Ireland's Son.. 55
The Seer of Kintail............ 56
Thidrek's Saga............ 15, 71
Thor 149, 151
Thorbjorg 50, 51, 52, 53, 54, 57, 79, 95, 100, 103, 110, 182, 183, 188, 192, 193
Thorsteinn's Saga 69
Triggers 19, 20, 87, 111, 112, 157, 188

U

Urd......................... 144, 147
Utiseta..... 35, 109, 130, 131, 132, 133

V

Vainamoinen .. 108, 174, 175
Valhalla 32, 33, 104, 106, 124, 129, 152, 172
Valkyries 102, 136, 150
Vanir . 34, 36, 148, 150, 151, 152
Vardlokkurs 45, 47, 59, 60, 63, 66, 87, 96, 97, 110, 111, 112, 113, 116, 120, 121, 135, 139, 160, 161, 173, 182, 184
Vatnsdoela Saga 54, 98, 103, 173
Veleda 57
Verdandi................. 144, 147
Vinland Sagas................ 164
Volsungasaga 15, 71, 95, 149, 178, 183
Voluspa ...31, 32, 33, 34, 35, 41, 42, 44, 45, 53, 54, 103, 106, 110, 111, 128, 175, 176, 190
Volva 13, 15, 31, 32, 33, 34, 35, 36, 37, 38, 39, 40, 41, 42, 43, 44, 45, 46, 47, 49, 50, 54, 55, 60, 63, 64, 69,

71, 79, 80, 81, 82, 83, 98,
99, 100, 103, 104, 109,
126, 129, 134, 146, 154,
164, 165, 176, 178, 189

W

Wyrd.........37, 143, 144, 153

Y

Yggdrasil 36, 62, 63, 64, 67,
77, 79, 83, 87, 88, 104,
111, 115, 119, 121, 151,
152, 160, 161, 182, 185,
189
Ynglingasaga.15, 65, 67, 69,
151, 173